LONDON'S BEST
Cocktail Bars

LONDON'S BEST
Cocktail Bars

The Most Popular
Hotspots

SUSAN COHEN

IMM lifestyle books

Read. Learn. Do What You Love.

Published 2019—IMM Lifestyle Books
http://foxchapelpublishing.co.uk

IMM Lifestyle Books are distributed in the UK by Grantham Book Service, Trent Road, Grantham, Lincolnshire, NG31 7XQ.

In North America, IMM Lifestyle Books are distributed by Fox Chapel Publishing, 903 Square Street, Mount Joy, PA 17552, *www.FoxChapelPublishing.com.*

ISBN 978-1-5048-0105-8

Library of Congress Cataloging-in-Publication Data

Names: Cohen, Susan, 1946- author.
Title: London's best cocktail bars / Susan Cohen.
Description: Mount Joy : IMM Lifestyle Books, 2019. | Includes index. |
   Identifiers: LCCN 2018059514 (print) | LCCN 2018060834 (ebook) | ISBN
   9781607656616 (ebook) | ISBN 9781504801058 (hardback)
Subjects: LCSH: Bars (Drinking establishments)—England—London—Guidebooks.
Classification: LCC TX950.59.G7 (ebook) | LCC TX950.59.G7 .C64 2019 (print) |
   DDC 647.95421—dc23
LC record available at https://lccn.loc.gov/2018059514

We are always looking for talented authors. To submit an idea, please send a brief inquiry to acquisitions@foxchapelpublishing.com.

Printed in China
10 9 8 7 6 5 4 3 2 1

Introduction

Exactly where and how the cocktail started is somewhat of a mystery; there are plenty of myths and legends around. Some say the name came from the practice of docking a horse's tail to show it was not a purebred. So, if you drank a cocktail, you were thought to be trying to elevate your social standing. Or maybe it comes from 'cock tailings', where the 'cock' was the tap of a barrel and the 'tails' were the dregs collected inside it. Regardless of whether either of these stories is true, there is a popular belief that the American cocktail is more than 200 years old, and that the martini, which author E. B. White called 'the elixir of quietude', has most definitely been around for more than 150 years. In fact, some of the best-known cocktails—the martini, the daiquiri, and the Manhattan—appeared between the 1860s and 1920, the year that Prohibition was introduced in America. For the next thirteen years, bootlegged alcohol and illegal drinking went underground into speakeasies, and as a result, bartenders became more inventive.

'Shaken, not stirred'. —James Bond

'*Happiness is…finding two olives in your martini when you're hungry*'. —*Johnny Carson*

Meanwhile, as transatlantic travel became more popular in the late 19th and early 20th centuries, cocktails reached our shores here in the UK. In response, many American bars opened up in London, with inspired bartenders serving these mixed or 'American' style drinks. Amongst the great names was The Savoy, who employed the first famous, and first female, bartender in 1903. Ada 'Coley' Coleman, whose signature cocktail was the Hanky Panky, took London by storm, and was followed by the inspirational Harry Craddock. He left America during Prohibition and in 1930 compiled *The Savoy Cocktail Book*, famously proclaiming cocktails to be 'the finest appetisers known'. His classic creations include the Corpse Reviver No. 2, one of the family of cocktails which are claimed to cure a hangover, and the Sherry Flip, made up simply of an egg yolk and sherry. Yet another classic cocktail bible, *The Official Mixer's Manual*, written by Patrick Gavin Duffy in 1934, included recipes for the improbable sounding Monkey Gland and Bosom Caresser.

When it comes to the cocktail party, British author Alec Waugh claimed responsibility for inventing this social gathering in 1925. He explained how he was looking for something to do between 5.30pm and 7.30pm, and so he invited some

friends to join him for drinks at his London home. But the English were devoted to tea, and he was disappointed when only one person turned up. Undeterred, he tried again in the autumn of 1925, and this time was economical with the truth, asking thirty people to tea at 5.00pm. They eagerly expected a cup of Earl Grey, but their hopes faded when, much to their amazement, Waugh produced his surprise in the form of 'a beaker of Daiquiris'. So, it seems, the cocktail party was born, and when Waugh returned from his next book tour, he found a nation where cocktails had replaced tea after 5.00pm.

> ## *'I never go jogging, it makes me spill my martini'.*
> ## *—George Burns*

Today, mixologists create exciting cocktails using the finest, and often unusual, natural ingredients sourced from near and far, and produce mixes which make the most of seasonal plants, herbs, and spices. Trends in cocktails are associated with different eras and can transport you to a different decade, from the 19th century through the Prohibition era and the Second World War to the Swinging Sixties. Hollywood films are loaded with cocktails—from the 1930s' *The Thin Man: Murder over Cocktails*, through Marilyn Monroe's Manhattan in *Some Like It Hot*, to Barbra

Streisand's 1968 green crème de menthe frappe in *Funny Girl*, to the Dude's White Russian in the 1998 film *The Big Lebowski*.

The bars in this guide are a selection of the best that London has to offer, from legendary sophisticated venues, to American bars, to themed spots and tiny speakeasies. There are places for a pre-theatre drink, places to unwind after a hard day at work, and places where you can spend time relaxing in quiet or not-so-quiet surroundings, depending on your mood. Some of the locations offer cocktail masterclasses so you can hone your skills and become a master of mixology. Others specialise in gin, vodka, or whisky-based cocktails, whilst champagne cocktails have many a follower, too. The bartenders in these establishments are devoted to their craft, and though they are always innovative, creating drinks to tickle the fancy, they still mix those eternal classics—for there are some cocktails that cannot and will not ever go out of fashion. The martini is a perfect example: the ingredients are simple, but it is hard to beat. From James Bond's widely recognized instruction that it be 'shaken not stirred', to Ernest Hemingway's declaration in *A Farewell to Arms*, 'I've never tasted anything so cool and clean. They made me feel civilized', this gin-based drink has been, and will continue to be, a star in the cocktail bible.

So, hit the streets of London with this book as your guide, and choose the bar that best suits your mood or takes your fancy; you won't be disappointed, and you'll definitely want to try as many of these unique, fun, and trendy places as you can.

Contents

Where applicable, venues are listed with the name
of the hotel in which they are located given.

Map of cocktail venues

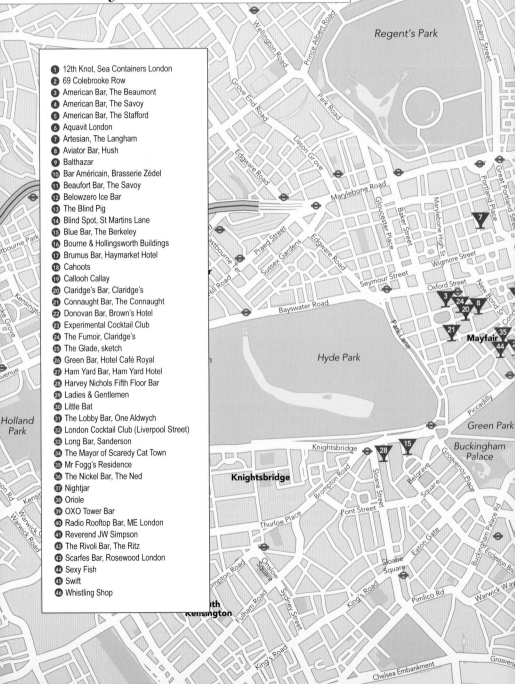

1. 12th Knot, Sea Containers London
2. 69 Colebrooke Row
3. American Bar, The Beaumont
4. American Bar, The Savoy
5. American Bar, The Stafford
6. Aquavit London
7. Artesian, The Langham
8. Aviator Bar, Hush
9. Balthazar
10. Bar Américain, Brasserie Zédel
11. Beaufort Bar, The Savoy
12. Belowzero Ice Bar
13. The Blind Pig
14. Blind Spot, St Martins Lane
15. Blue Bar, The Berkeley
16. Bourne & Hollingsworth Buildings
17. Brumus Bar, Haymarket Hotel
18. Cahoots
19. Calooh Callay
20. Claridge's Bar, Claridge's
21. Connaught Bar, The Connaught
22. Donovan Bar, Brown's Hotel
23. Experimental Cocktail Club
24. The Fumoir, Claridge's
25. The Glade, sketch
26. Green Bar, Hotel Café Royal
27. Ham Yard Bar, Ham Yard Hotel
28. Harvey Nichols Fifth Floor Bar
29. Ladies & Gentlemen
30. Little Bat
31. The Lobby Bar, One Aldwych
32. London Cocktail Club (Liverpool Street)
33. Long Bar, Sanderson
34. The Mayor of Scaredy Cat Town
35. Mr Fogg's Residence
36. The Nickel Bar, The Ned
37. Nightjar
38. Oriole
39. OXO Tower Bar
40. Radio Rooftop Bar, ME London
41. Reverend JW Simpson
42. The Rivoli Bar, The Ritz
43. Scarfes Bar, Rosewood London
44. Sexy Fish
45. Swift
46. Whistling Shop

12TH KNOT

Sea Containers London

Whizz up in the lift (elevator) to the 12th floor of the South Bank's Sea Containers London, and you are in the right place for 12th Knot, the hotel's rooftop bar, which affords guests striking views across the River Thames and London's skyline. It is stylish, light, and airy during the day, with a real outdoor/indoor garden feel about it. Lush plants, plush mauve banquettes, comfy armchairs and lounge spaces, glittering chandeliers, and a very shiny gold bar all add to the luxe feel. As wonderful as it is during the day, the place truly comes alive once it gets to sunset and later, and has a more bling feel about it.

The carefully curated cocktails are British and American inspired, aimed at blending the best of the two cultures, with a transatlantic mix of tastes and flavours. You can, of course, ask one of the team to mix your favourite. Depending on when

ADDRESS:
Sea Containers London, 20 Upper Ground, South Bank, London SE1 9PD

TEL: +44 (0)20 3747 1063

EMAIL: 12thknot@seacontainers london.com

WEB: www.seacontainerslondon .com/food-drink/12th-knot

OPENING HOURS:
Tuesday and Wednesday 5.00pm–1.00am, Thursday to Saturday 5.00pm–1.30am. Outdoor terrace open 5.00pm–10.00pm. Closed Sunday and Monday.

BOOKINGS:
Via the website; walk-ins are first come, first served. Check the website calendar for closures due to private events.

DRESS CODE:
Smart casual; no sportswear, trainers/ sneakers, or flip-flops

AGE RESTRICTION: 21+

NEAREST UNDERGROUND STATIONS:
Waterloo, Blackfriars

PLACES OF INTEREST NEARBY: Tate Modern, River Thames, Shakespeare's Globe, Borough Market, National Theatre, OXO Tower

you visit, you might find Thanks a Tot, a gift for anyone with a love of the sea. This mix of three rums, with the addition of cinnamon and pimento, hopped peach drops, citrus, and caraway, is rich and full of flavour, and both sour and aromatic. From across the Atlantic, there's Coquetier, which comes with a warning to sip slowly. This is for you if you like your spirits dark, for it's a complex and strong drink, made of cognac, the spicy, fruity French liqueur Suze Saveur d'Autrefois, the Italian bitter liqueur Cynar, Bulleit Rye whiskey, Heering cherry liqueur, claret, Peychaud's, and orange bitters. A small bar food menu has good poké bowls to share. You can't miss the buzz and vibe here, especially from 7.00pm on Wednesday nights when Skyline sessions feature live music, or from Thursday to Sunday when the DJs are in action.

69 COLEBROOKE ROW

L ook out for the lantern above the door of this tiny speakeasy-style bar on the corner of a backstreet in Islington. 69 Colebrooke Row, also known as The Bar with No Name, is a wow of a place, and you really need to make a reservation, or prepare to be disappointed. Inside it's 1950s Italian café style, relaxed and cosy, and the staff are smartly dressed in the 69 Colebrooke Row jacket with distinctive logo, white shirt, black tie, trousers, and shoes. The menu is the creation of cocktail supremo Tony Conigliaro and his pioneering team at the research and development laboratory at The Drink Factory. The original, seasonally changing cocktails are created using secret ingredients that, in careful combination, result in drinks that challenge the senses in equal measure without being gimmicky. 69's Death in Venice cocktail recipe makes a particularly refreshing tipple, simply prepared with Campari, Prosecco, and

ADDRESS: 69 Colebrooke Row, Islington, London N1 8AA

TEL: +44 (0)7540 528593

EMAIL: drinks@69colebrookerow.com

WEB: www.69colebrookerow.com

OPENING HOURS:
Sunday to Wednesday 5.00pm–midnight, Thursday 5.00pm–1.00am, Friday and Saturday 5.00pm–2.00am

BOOKINGS:
Available for parties of 1–8 guests, for one hour; visit www.exploretock.com/69colebrookerow. You can ask for a longer time slot. Walk-ins welcome.

AGE RESTRICTION: 18+

EVENTS/LIVE MUSIC:
For the Sunday night programme, check www.69colebrookerow.com/events. The in-house pianist plays on Tuesday and Thursday evenings, 8.00pm–11.00pm.

MASTERCLASSES:
Check the website for Saturday and Sunday afternoon dates and details: www.69colebrookerow.com/masterclasses/#masterclass-details

NEAREST UNDERGROUND STATIONS:
Angel, Highbury & Islington

PLACES OF INTEREST NEARBY:
Exmouth Market, Sadler's Wells Theatre, Victoria Miro Gallery, Gagosian Gallery, Clockmakers' Museum, Postal Museum, London Canal Museum

homemade grapefruit bitters. For a real treat, or even a challenge, don't miss the bar's own innovative version of the ultimate 19th-century hangover cure, the Prairie Oyster, which you must drink all at once! It's a wonder of modern invention how the traditional raw egg yolk has been replaced by a 'tomato' yolk, and instead of Worcestershire sauce, there's horseradish vodka and Oloroso sherry, shallots, pepper sauce, celery salt, and oyster leaf. If you prefer, classic and non-alcoholic cocktails are available on request. The place is always animated, but on the nights that the in-house pianist is there, it positively vibrates to the beat. A tiny neighbourhood bar with a big heart.

AMERICAN BAR

Who would ever guess that this swanky American bar has only been here since The Beaumont opened in 2014? Situated on a quiet garden square a stone's throw from Selfridges, the listed Art Deco façade of the building dates back to 1926, and the interior is a modern creation that recaptures the glamour of the 1920s, when cocktails travelled across the Atlantic and found a captive audience in London. The American Bar—also known as Jimmy's—is open all day from 11.30am and is small enough to be intimate without being claustrophobic. It's a handsome bar with an old-fashioned feel, and the décor, like the cocktails, is the epitome of elegance, from the herringbone parquet flooring to the dark leather booths, mirrored bar, and glass-and-bronze chandelier. The sober walnut-panelled walls display monochrome studio portraits of early 20th-century celebrities and Hollywood legends, taken by a galaxy of famous photographers, including Cecil Beaton, and adding a touch of theatricality.

ADDRESS:
The Beaumont, 8 Balderton Street, Mayfair, London W1K 6TF

TEL:
+44 (0)20 7499 1001

EMAIL:
info@thebeaumont.com

WEB:
www.thebeaumont.com/dining/american-bar

OPENING HOURS:
Monday to Saturday 11.30am–midnight, Sunday 11.30am–11.00pm

BOOKINGS:
Not taken

AGE RESTRICTION:
Alcohol only served to 18+. Children under 16 permitted in the bar until 6.00pm.

NEAREST UNDERGROUND STATIONS:
Bond Street

PLACES OF INTEREST NEARBY:
The Wallace Collection, Oxford Street, Bond Street, Apsley House, Hyde Park, Speakers' Corner

The service is equally old-school, personal and friendly, and the cocktails, served in Art Deco glasses, are classic, strictly shaken or stirred. This is a bar that would have found favour with Ernest Hemingway and F. Scott Fitzgerald. Choose your tipple from one of the four groups, with the emphasis on champagne, bourbon/rye whiskey, gin/vodka/tequila, and rum/cognac, and expect to find the timeless daiquiri, martini, and old fashioned on the long list. The signature champagne cocktail is The Beaumont, a heady, satisfying blend of champagne, gin, dry sherry, elderflower, pineapple, and lemon, and the eponymous Jimmy's own version of The Collins is made with Finlandia vodka, lemon juice, sugar, and soda. There is no list of non-alcoholic cocktails, but the bar staff will happily mix up anything you fancy. Expect complimentary olives and nuts, regularly refilled, and, if you are lingering longer, try a bar meal or casual snack, in which case don't miss the popcorn chicken. A truly iconic bar.

AMERICAN BAR

The Savoy

The iconic Art Deco bar at The Savoy is the longest surviving of the American cocktail bars in London. When the bar opened in 1893, it was in the original riverside part of the hotel, but it moved to its current location in 1904. Amongst its claims to fame was the appointment of Ada 'Coley' Coleman, who arrived there in 1903 and became the first female bartender. Harry Craddock followed in her footsteps, inspiring generations of mixologists with his classic inventions and publishing them in *The Savoy Cocktail Book*, which is still in print to consult today. Many historical events have been marked here, including the first moon landing in 1969, when barman Joe Gilmore created his own tribute to the astronauts. Neil Armstrong's story is that Gilmore's cocktail Moon Walk, a mix of Grand Marnier and grapefruit juice topped up with champagne and rose water, was his first drink when he was allowed out of quarantine. This was thanks to The Savoy, who had dispatched it in a flask to America.

ADDRESS:
The Savoy, 100 Strand, Covent Garden, London WC2R 0EZ

TEL: +44 (0)20 7836 4343

EMAIL: savoy@fairmont.com

WEB: www.fairmont.com/savoy-london/dining/americanbar

OPENING HOURS:
Monday to Saturday 11.30am–midnight, Sunday 12.00pm–11.00pm

BOOKINGS: Not taken

DRESS CODE:
Smart casual; no sportswear

AGE RESTRICTION: 18+

EVENTS/LIVE MUSIC:
Daily 6.30pm–11.30pm, till 10.30pm Sunday

MASTERCLASSES:
Visit www.fairmont.com/savoy-london/promotions/culinaryevents, call +44 (0)20 7420 2111, or email savoy@fairmont.com

NEAREST UNDERGROUND STATIONS:
Covent Garden, Charing Cross, Embankment

PLACES OF INTEREST NEARBY: Somerset House, The Courtauld Gallery and Institute of Art, Royal Festival Hall, National Theatre, Savoy Theatre, Covent Garden, Royal Opera House, London Transport Museum, London Film Museum, Cinema Museum

Then, as now, there is a generosity about the bar, with welcoming, unobtrusive staff, white-jacketed mixologists, complimentary trays of peanuts, crackers, and olives that are constantly replenished, and a small but indulgent menu of bar snacks from oysters to smoked salmon. The walls are adorned with 1960s and 70s black and white celebrity portraits by Terry O'Neill, the seating is comfortable and relaxed, and the bar does what The Savoy does best: gives you the style and the glamour of a bygone era. You

can enjoy live music and entertainment every night from 6.30pm, and you can be sure that whatever cocktail you choose will be perfectly mixed, created with great care, and impeccably presented. Ada Coleman, Harry Cradock, and Joe Gilmore all have their place in the vintage list with their respective unique cocktails: Hanky Panky, White Lady, and Moon Walk. Cocktail invention here has endured through the ages, with a themed cocktail menu that changes annually; past themes have been variously inspired by London's iconic buildings, by Britain's coastline and landscape, and by the amazing collection of Terry O'Neill's photographs. Do check the website to see what wonderful cocktail collection is current. The American Bar manages to be avant-garde but still retain its historic reputation as one of London's landmark bars and great institutions, and it should definitely not be missed.

Hanky Panky

Recipe courtesy of Ada Coleman/American Bar at The Savoy

Ada Coleman, The Savoy's first female bartender, invented this twist on a sweet martini in 1903. The traditional dry vermouth is replaced by sweet, and just a few drops of the herby, bitter, not-so-secret ingredient, Fernet-Branca, transforms it into a new drink.

INGREDIENTS

- 45ml (1½ oz) Bombay Sapphire gin
- 45ml (1½ oz) Punt e Mes vermouth
- 7.5ml (¼ oz) Fernet-Branca herbal liqueur
- Orange peel

METHOD

Stir all the liquid ingredients and strain into a signature martini glass. Garnish with orange peel.

This recipe presents measurements for both UK and US readers. Units are given first for UK readers in the original measurement units, then for US readers in converted units in parentheses. Do not mix the units.

AMERICAN BAR

The Stafford

The legendary American Bar at The Stafford has a faithful clientele who love its blend of English tradition and contemporary sophistication. This is a place where you can meet a friend, have a discreet meeting or lively conversation, relax after work, or stop for a drink before dinner. The atmosphere is clubby, cosy, and comfortable, with intimate corners. There is memorabilia everywhere, with photographs of the galaxy of British and American celebrities who have frequented this stylish bar adorning the mahogany wood-panelled walls.

The bar, which serves signature and classic drinks, is supervised by Benoit Provost, whose skill at creating new as well as updated vintage cocktails has earned him an enviable reputation. His 'Journey Through St James's' cocktail list does just what it says in the name, following a winding path around the hidden passageways and corners of the area and revealing a wealth of local tales. The Godolphin is a perfect example,

ADDRESS:
The Stafford, 16–18 St James's Place,
St James's, London SW1A 1NJ

TEL:
+44 (0)20 7518 1234

EMAIL:
reservations@thegamebird.com

WEB:
www.thestaffordlondon.com/
the-american-bar

OPENING HOURS:
Monday to Saturday 8.00am–
midnight (1.00am for hotel guests),
Sunday 8.00am–midnight

BOOKINGS:
Tables can be booked inside from
8.00am to 3.00pm. Outside tables are
first come, first served.

DRESS CODE:
Smart casual

AGE RESTRICTION:
18+

**NEAREST UNDERGROUND
STATIONS:**
Green Park

**PLACES OF
INTEREST NEARBY:**
Green Park, Buckingham Palace, St
James's Palace, Royal Academy of
Arts, Bond Street, Piccadilly

for it is named after the aristocratic philanthropist Francis Godolphin, whose house once stood where the hotel's coach house is now. It's an intriguing mix of Woodford Reserve, red wine infused with berries and cinnamon, lemon juice, and egg white. Meanwhile, The QM combines Tanqueray No. Ten, Brillet pear liqueur, Bénédictine, and Dubonnet, and was, apparently, much favoured by Queen Elizabeth The Queen Mother, who visited from time to time.

There is a terrific, very comprehensive food menu, full of exciting Mediterranean inspired dishes, from snacks to sandwiches to small plates to large plates and charcuterie, so there is something for everyone. This American bar is a hidden treasure and, besides oozing atmosphere, has terrific drinks, all of which are served with panache.

AQUAVIT LONDON

Grab a seat at the gorgeous marble-topped bar at this Michelin-starred restaurant in St James's and you can enjoy a unique Aquavit house cocktail created by the talented bar team. The bar has one of the largest selections of the famed Scandi spirit in the UK; in case you are not familiar with it, aquavit is a little bit like gin without the juniper berries and is quite delicious served neat. You'll find Nordic-inspired cocktails created using O.P. Anderson, the original Swedish aquavit that has been around for over 125 years, a clean-tasting spirit seasoned with caraway, anise, and fennel. Other cocktails feature the newer and milder, slightly sweet and fruity 1986 Hallands Fläder.

The Aquavit cocktail menu has a number of core cocktails that will always be on the menu, but there are also seasonal changes. You might get to try the highball Fika It Out, a play on the Swedish tradition of coffee and cake, which combines cinnamon bun, milk-washed O.P. Anderson, and soda. Or, for a clean, invigorating, light drink,

and a variation on a classic, look no further than the Apple Gimlet. No lime here, but instead you have apple cordial combined with O.P. Anderson Klar aquavit and 30/40 eau de vie. If you are there for breakfast, then don't miss the morning cocktails, including Viking Breakfast, a Nordic version of a Bloody Mary, which is made of aquavit, tomato juice, soy sauce, balsamic vinegar, dill, horseradish, and a spicy mix. And what better accompaniment to your Aquavit cocktail than a not-to-be-missed smorgasbord? For a real treat, try the Vendace roe 'Kalix Löjrom', a delicacy of Swedish caviar topped with diced red onion, sour cream—you may have had it before with crème fraîche— and snipped chives. The Scandis have got it just right.

ADDRESS:
St James's Market, 1 Carlton Street, St James's, London SW1Y 4QQ

TEL:
+44 (0)20 7024 9848

EMAIL:
info@aquavitrestaurants.com

WEB:
www.aquavitrestaurants.com/london

OPENING HOURS:
The bar is licensed until 1.00am. The restaurant serves Monday to Friday 7.30am–11.00pm, Saturday 11.00am–11.30pm, Sunday 11.00am–10.30pm

BOOKINGS:
Not taken for the bar, but available for the restaurant

DRESS CODE:
Smart casual, cool and chic

AGE RESTRICTION:
18+ in the bar area

MASTERCLASSES:
Selected Mondays from 6.30pm–7.30pm

NEAREST UNDERGROUND STATIONS:
Piccadilly Circus, Charing Cross

PLACES OF INTEREST NEARBY:
St James's Park, Downing Street, Royal Academy, Institute of Contemporary Arts, National Portrait Gallery, National Gallery

Chanterelle

Recipe courtesy of Aquavit London

The bar manager at Aquavit London describes this drink as an elegant cocktail, strong and complex, dry with some nutty notes. The chanterelle is pickled, which also cuts through the savory flavours of the martini. It's one to be enjoyed and adored.

INGREDIENTS

- 50ml (2 oz) Løitens Three Star aquavit
- 12.5ml (½ oz) Cocchi Americano aromatized wine
- 12.5ml (½ oz) Manzanilla wine
- Pickled chanterelle

METHOD

Stir liquid ingredients and serve straight up.
Garnish with a pickled chanterelle.

This recipe presents measurements for both UK and US readers. Units are given first for UK readers in the original measurement units, then for US readers in converted units in parentheses. Do not mix the units.

ARTESIAN

The Langham

A rtesian takes its name from the 110-metre (360-foot) artesian well that lies beneath the foundations and that supplied the original hotel with the purest water in London. It's a world apart, a truly sophisticated venue that nevertheless has a fun atmosphere that ensures an enjoyable and memorable visit. There is music, but it's never too loud to drown the conversation, so it makes the perfect date venue, place to unwind after work, or spot to enjoy a tipple before an evening meal or the theatre; it is equally wonderful for a nightcap. The room is chic and glamorous, decorated in a modern oriental style, with mile-high ceilings, Doric columns, mirrored wall panels, and chandeliers, plus the benefit of very comfortable seating. The service is discreet and professional, with lovely waitstaff—Team Artesian—who really know their business. There's some people watching to be done here, and as the bar is across

ADDRESS:
The Langham, 1c Portland Place,
Regent Street, Marylebone, London
W1B 1JA

TEL:
+44 (0)20 7636 1000

EMAIL:
info@artesian-bar.co.uk

WEB:
www.artesian-bar.co.uk

OPENING HOURS:
Monday to Saturday 11.00am–last
call 1.30am, Sunday 11.00am–last
call 11.30pm

BOOKINGS:
Available except for Fridays and
Saturdays

DRESS CODE:
Smart casual

AGE RESTRICTION:
18+ after 6.00pm

**NEAREST UNDERGROUND
STATIONS:**
Oxford Circus, Regent's Park, Bond
Street

**PLACES OF
INTEREST NEARBY:**
BBC Broadcasting House, Royal
Institute of British Architects, The
Photographers Gallery, Regent's
Park, Regent Street, Oxford Street,
Bond Street

the road from the BBC, you may well see a few
familiar media faces amongst the guests.

The theme for the showstopping cocktails
changes every year: in the past, 'Surrealism' was
influenced by the master of art Salvadore Dali,
whilst 'Perception', another theme, aimed at
challenging your expectations of a cocktail.
More recently, 'Artesian Moments' has been the
theme, with cocktails created to remind you
of important highlights in your life as well as
the fragrances and flavours you associate with
them. If themed cocktails don't float your boat,
then the bar staff are more than happy to mix
you a martini, perfectly crisp and clean, or any
other favourite. The complimentary nibbles are
great, and are constantly replenished, and the
bar food is, like the cocktails, a cut above the
rest. Artesian has a reputation for being a lively
place, not in the least fussy, and is just as good
for a stop after shopping or a business meeting
as it is for a party or a date.

AVIATOR BAR

Possibly one of London's best kept secrets, Aviator Bar at Hush is as exciting as it is surprising. Finding the place is the only challenge you will face, for it's tucked away in a hidden courtyard off New Bond Street's Brook Street, reached by walking down a cobbled lane in the historic heart of Mayfair. Cross the glorious courtyard and, once inside, follow the elegant curved staircase upstairs to Aviator. Choose a cosy, comfortable corner, grab a seat by the windows, or stake your claim at the bar, and settle down to work your way through the extensive menu.

The team has created some thirty cocktails, all inspired by the golden age of air travel. Of course, you don't have to leave your seat to be transported on a cocktail journey around the world, for the bar's talented, award-winning mixologists will do all the legwork for you. Innovation and fun are the name of the game, with plenty of puns on the way. You'll find 'American Expedition' cocktails featuring Head in

ADDRESS:
Hush, 8 Lancashire Court, Brook
Street, Mayfair, London W1S 1EY

TEL:
+44 (0)20 7659 1500

EMAIL:
info@hush.co.uk

WEB:
www.hush.co.uk/aviator-bar-at-hush

OPENING HOURS:
Monday to Saturday 12.00pm–
midnight. Closed Sunday.

BOOKINGS:
Via the website, email, or phone

AGE RESTRICTION:
18+ after 7.00pm

MASTERCLASSES:
Inquire via the website or contact
events@hush.co.uk

**NEAREST UNDERGROUND
STATIONS:**
Bond Street, Oxford Circus

**PLACES OF
INTEREST NEARBY:**
Bond Street, Regent Street, Handel
& Hendrix in London, Grays
Antique Centre, Royal Academy of
Arts, Wigmore Hall, The Wallace
Collection

the Game, created from Canada's quadruple-
distilled Crystal Head vodka, with violet
liqueur, Luc Belaire rosé, fresh apple juice, and
berries. The decorative garnish of an ice puck
is a tribute to the national winter sport, whilst
the glass is a cleverly recycled and decorated,
if a little weird, Crystal Head bottle. Prefer
an 'Island in the Sun'? Then try Bon Vivant,
and enjoy the good living of the French-
Caribbean island of Martinique with a drink
combining the warm caramel, exotic spice, and
dried fruit aromas of Clément V.S.O.P. with
Campari, The King's Ginger, Oloroso sherry,
and Angostura bitters. There are plenty more
tantalising combinations, and amongst the

six 'Bartender's Favourites', you'll find two takes on the traditional martini. If you want to stay grounded, then you have four excellent non-alcoholic cocktails to choose from, or you can have a favourite made up for you. There's a good selection of bites, from nibbles to light bites or something more substantial, all served with style.

If you are thinking of having a small party—fifteen people max—then book the Concorde Room, a more private space just off the main bar. And for a real treat, why not organise a cocktail masterclass, and from your seat behind the bar let the skilled team guide you through making your own cocktails?

Romani Rose
(Bulgaria)

Recipe courtesy of Aviator Bar at Hush

Life's a bed of roses with these botanical flavours and Hendrick's Gin, created by infusing this unusually smooth gin with the remarkable Bulgarian *Rosa damascena* and specially selected cucumbers.

INGREDIENTS

- 40ml (1½ oz) Hendrick's gin
- 15ml (½ oz) elderflower cordial
- 15ml (½ oz) O.P. Anderson aquavit
- 10ml (2 tsp) lime juice
- Top off with homemade rosebud soda water
- Cucumber
- Edible flowers
- Crushed rosebud

METHOD

Build the drink in a flowerpot with cubed ice. Garnish with cucumber, edible flowers, and a crushed rosebud.

This recipe presents measurements for both UK and US readers. Units are given first for UK readers in the original measurement units, then for US readers in converted units in parentheses. Do not mix the units.

BALTHAZAR

The famed original Balthazar opened in Soho in downtown New York in spring 1997, but London had to wait until early 2013 for the only other branch outside of Manhattan to finally hit the capital city. Right in the heart of Covent Garden and Theatreland, this restaurant occupies a heritage building that was once home to the Covent Garden Flower Cellars, where the market traders kept their stock, and then housed the old theatre museum. It is perfectly placed for a cocktail any day of the week from around midday. So if you are taking a break from exploring the area, en route to the theatre or opera, needing a break from shopping, or simply fancy a drink, this is an ideal spot. The interior décor is ornate but retains the feel of a typical French brasserie, from the zinc bar, brass rails, and red banquette seating to the bustling atmosphere.

ADDRESS:
4–6 Russell Street, Covent Garden,
London WC2B 5HZ

TEL:
+44 (0)20 3301 1155

EMAIL:
info@balthazarlondon.com

WEB:
www.balthazarlondon.com

OPENING HOURS:
Cocktails served Monday to
Thursday 11.00am–11.30pm, Friday
11.30am–midnight, Saturday
11.30am–midnight, Sunday
11.30am–11.00pm. Manhattan Hour
10.00pm to close.

BOOKINGS:
Visit https://balthazarlondon.
capricebookings.com

AGE RESTRICTION:
18+

**NEAREST UNDERGROUND
STATIONS:**
Covent Garden

**PLACES OF
INTEREST NEARBY:**
London Film Museum, Covent
Garden, Royal Opera House,
London Transport Museum, Theatre
Royal Drury Lane, Lyceum Theatre,
Fortune Theatre, Savoy Theatre,
Somerset House

House cocktails, created by cocktail king Brian Silva, include a Golden Negroni, a mix of Beefeater gin, Campari, Cinzano Orancio, and G. Miclo Poire Williams, and the Screaming Viking, concocted from Tequila Ocho, Swedish punsch, Martini Fiero, and lime. If you are visiting for weekend brunch, then there is an additional list of cocktails, including the Peach Bellini, Buck's Fizz, and Balthazar's Bloody Mary, which contains Belvedere vodka and the restaurant's bespoke blend of juice and spice. There's also a good selection of no-booze cocktails for teetotallers. A new addition in autumn 2018 were the 'Manhattan Hour' cocktails, with each well-priced interpretation of whiskey, vermouth, bitters, and garnish inspired by a different New York district. You could try Harlem, mixed from Maker's Mark 46, Cocchi Americano, Cynar, and orange bitters, or enjoy Hell's Kitchen, made from Sazerac rye whiskey, Byyrh, Montenegro, and barrel-aged bitters. Whiskey lovers will find a select list of six American whiskey cocktails on the drinks menu—besides which there are 160 different American whiskies from more than fifteen US states, as well as blended and single malts. If you are unable to book a bar seat and book a table instead, you'll have to order from the food menu as well. And if you want to be your own mixologist, don't leave without buying a copy of Brian Silva's book, *Mixing in the Right Circles*.

BAR AMÉRICAIN

Brasserie Zédel

Bar Américain is one of four spaces at Brasserie Zédel, and is just the place to finish your workday or start your evening, right in the heart of London's Theatreland. The brasserie itself has an interesting background, for it used to be part of the Regent Palace Hotel, which, when it opened in 1915, was the largest hotel in Europe with an incredible 1,028 bedrooms. The bar is in the basement, and as you walk down the stairs, take a look at the wonderful photographs that adorn the walls, showcasing jazz pianists and musicians of a past era. The elegant lounge has original art deco fittings and retains the glamour of the 1920s and 30s, when jazz was all the rage. The lighting is low and relaxing, the seating a mix of leather banquette seating and tables and chairs, and the background jazz music adds to the great ambience.

ADDRESS:
Brasserie Zédel, 20 Sherwood Street, Soho, London W1F 7ED

TEL:
+44 (0)20 7734 4888

EMAIL:
info@brasseriezedel.com

WEB:
www.brasseriezedel.com/bar-americain

OPENING HOURS:
Monday to Wednesday 1.00pm–midnight, Thursday to Saturday 1.00pm–1.00am (last entry midnight), Sunday 1.00pm–11.00pm

BOOKINGS:
Not taken

AGE RESTRICTION:
18+

NEAREST UNDERGROUND STATIONS:
Piccadilly Circus

PLACES OF INTEREST NEARBY:
Theatreland, Soho, Regent Street, Trafalgar Square, Piccadilly, Trocadero Entertainment Centre

Whilst you are deciding what to drink, tuck into the complimentary dish of smoky popcorn and take a look at the snack menu, which offers reasonably priced bowl food such as crispy fried chicken and deep fried prawns. The cocktail menu pays homage to post–World War One America and France and features classic and more inventive house cocktails. You can enjoy, amongst others, a classic old fashioned or a Hemingway Daiquiri, which takes its inspiration and name from the novelist Ernest Hemingway. He lived in Havana in the 1930s, where the El Floridita bar was a popular local haunt. The story goes that he saw the bartender mixing daiquiris and asked to try one, commenting that he

preferred his with twice the rum and no sugar. The bartender duly mixed the drink to this recipe, and so this daiquiri acquired its eponymous name. House cocktails at Bar Américain include Lazy River, made from Portobello Road gin, Lillet Blanc, Byrrh, Campari, and grapefruit bitters, and Lindy Hop, a cocktail of Finlandia vodka, lychee liqueur, orgeat, apple juice, and lemon juice. The story goes that this was named after Charles Lindbergh's daring solo flight across the Atlantic from New York to Paris in 1927, when one newspaper headline read 'Lindy hops off for Paris'. There's no need to travel abroad, though, for you are bound to find something to tickle your fancy here.

Old Fashioned

Recipe courtesy of Bar Américain at Brasserie Zédel

An old fashioned is just that, and has changed its name over the years from the original title, whisky cocktail. When Jerry Thomas wrote *The Bar-Tender's Guide* in 1862, he included a 'wine-glass of whiskey' in the recipe, which, before the days of bourbon, was most likely rye. He instructed that his cocktail should be shaken, but today's bartenders insist that the drink should be stirred, and stirred, and stirred some more. The drink is traditionally served in a short, round, tumbler-like glass that is named after the drink.

INGREDIENTS

- 60ml (2 oz) bourbon
- 5ml (1 tsp) sugar syrup
- 1 dash Angostura bitters
- 2 dashes orange bitters
- Orange zest

METHOD

Stir all of the liquid ingredients together in a rocks glass with cubed ice. To finish, garnish with the zest of an orange.

This recipe presents measurements for both UK and US readers. Units are given first for UK readers in the original measurement units, then for US readers in converted units in parentheses. Do not mix the units.

BEAUFORT BAR

The Savoy boasts two beautiful bars, with the Beaufort Bar, tucked away off the Thames Foyer, the more intimate, romantic of them. The black-and-gold colour scheme and candlelight create a romantic ambience, so this is an ideal place for a date, and if you are seated in one of the gilded alcoves, you are in a prime position to people watch. There is a theatrical, glamorous feel about the actual bar, which is set back on the far side of the room, a reflection of its former life as the hotel's cabaret stage. Stage curtain drapes add to the drama, but instead of the tail-coated and bow-tied members of the Savoy bands who used to play here, and the famous names, including George Gershwin, who graced the stage, there are experienced mixologists creating wonderful cocktails.

The list is extensive, from the exclusive 'Vintage and Rare' section, which includes The Dubonnet Cocktail, a favourite of the late Queen Mother, to the current themed

menu, which changes seasonally. Whatever journey you are taken on, you can be sure the cocktails will be masterpieces of invention, created with skill, using the finest ingredients, and providing you with a sensory experience to savor. To add to your enjoyment, you can sip your cocktails to the sound of live music, which drifts in from the adjoining Thames Foyer. The hotel has a reputation for being a mecca for the rich and famous, and the Beaufort Bar is a celebration of a bygone era. Add some delicious bar food and you are in for a super and memorable evening.

ADDRESS:
The Savoy, 100 Strand, Covent Garden, London WC2R 0EZ

TEL: +44 (0)20 7420 2111

EMAIL: savoy@fairmont.com

WEB: www.fairmont.com/savoy-london/dining/beaufortbar

OPENING HOURS:
Monday to Saturday
5.00pm–1.00am; last call 12.30am.
Closed Sunday.

BOOKINGS:
Available for Monday to Thursday only; call between 9.00am–8.00pm or email

DRESS CODE:
Smart casual; no sportswear

AGE RESTRICTION: 18+

EVENTS/LIVE MUSIC:
Daily 6.30pm–11.30pm

NEAREST UNDERGROUND STATIONS:
Covent Garden, Charing Cross, Embankment

PLACES OF INTEREST NEARBY:
Somerset House, The Courtauld Gallery and Institute of Art, Royal Festival Hall, National Theatre, Savoy Theatre, Covent Garden, Royal Opera House, London Transport Museum, London Film Museum, Cinema Museum

BELOWZERO ICE BAR

You may not think that having a cocktail at -5°C (23°F) is your idea of fun, but believe me, this is an experience not to be missed. Belowzero has the accolade of being the only permanent ice bar in the UK, so it really is a unique place. It's family friendly during the daytime, so it's a fun place to take the children. Everything in the bar, from the walls to the furniture to the impressive ice sculptures, is made of crystal clear ice from Sweden's River Torne, making it London's coolest venue in every sense of the word. The theme changes—a recent one was a tongue-in-cheek tribute to London—so you can return again and again and find a completely different set of sculptures.

When you make a reservation, you get a fixed session of 40 minutes, and on arrival, you and the other people in the same time slot will be decked out in a cosy cape and

ADDRESS:
31–33 Heddon Street, Mayfair,
London W1B 4BN

TEL:
+44 (0)20 7478 8910

EMAIL:
res@belowzerolondon.com

WEB:
www.belowzeroicebar.com

OPENING HOURS:
Monday 2.15pm–10.15pm, Tuesday
to Thursday 1.30pm–11.00pm,
Friday 1.30pm–12.30am, Saturday
10.30am–12.30am, Sunday
12.00pm–10.15pm. Fixed session
times of 40 minutes.

BOOKINGS: Visit https://reserve
.belowzeroicebar.com

DRESS CODE:
None; warm outerwear provided

AGE RESTRICTION:
Minors are welcome during
daytime sessions, last entry 6.30pm
Monday to Saturday, Sunday all day.
Otherwise strictly 18+. Free entry to
children 8 and under, drinks extra.

**NEAREST UNDERGROUND
STATIONS:**
Oxford Circus, Piccadilly Circus

**PLACES OF
INTEREST NEARBY:**
Theatreland, Soho, Regent Street,
Trafalgar Square, Piccadilly,
Trocadero Entertainment Centre

gloves to keep you warm, and enter the ice
bar together. Your drink is served in a unique
glass that is designed to keep it perfectly
chilled. Cocktails are grouped according to
their base: vodka, bourbon, gin, rum, or tequila.
You might like to try the grapefruit Negroni,
a citrusy mix of gin and Martini Rosso with
blood orange purée and pink grapefruit juice,
or the Belowzero take on a margarita, mixing
Olmeca Altos tequila with blue curaçao, tonic,
and lemon juice. There are a couple of delicious
non-alcoholic numbers, as well as Prosecco and
champagne cocktails, although these carry a
supplemental charge.

When your icy session is over, you can move
to the comfortable warm cocktail bar on the
ground floor, which serves excellent bar snacks,
including terrific halloumi chips. If you want
something more, then head downstairs to the
restaurant, which serves modern British cuisine.

THE BLIND PIG

J ust to make it clear, this Soho speakeasy, hidden away above Jason Atherton's
Social Eating House, has nothing at all to do with a pig that can't see. The truth
is that during the Prohibition era, 'Blind Pig' was one of the names used in America
for an illicit bar. Look out for the unremarkable entrance on Poland Street and the
blindfolded little pig that does double duty as a doorknocker. Upstairs you'll find
a retro, low-lit interior with a vintage twist. There are antique mirrored ceilings, a
copper-topped bar, leather banquette seating, and reclaimed, mismatched wooden
chairs that all come together to create a comfortable, understated, relaxed vibe.

The cocktails are far from low key, though. The flavours are clever and the
presentation unique, with a menu that takes its humour and ideas from across a
range of well-known children's stories, from Peter Rabbit to Harry Potter, with puns
everywhere. What Beatrix Potter would make of Jemima Puddleduck's Fowl Play,

ADDRESS: 58 Poland Street, Soho, London W1F 7NR

TEL: +44 (0)20 7993 3251

EMAIL: N/A

WEB: www.socialeatinghouse.com

OPENING HOURS: Monday to Thursday 12.00pm–11.30pm, Friday and Saturday 12.00pm–midnight. Closed Sunday.

BOOKINGS: Via phone, but not essential; walk-ins welcome

AGE RESTRICTION: 18+

NEAREST UNDERGROUND STATIONS: Oxford Circus, Tottenham Court Road

PLACES OF INTEREST NEARBY: Soho, Chinatown, Theatreland, National Portrait Gallery, National Gallery

created from duck fat–washed Aylesbury Duck vodka, blood orange, Chartreuse, honey, herbs, and spices, is anyone's guess. No doubt Paddington Bear, who travelled from darkest Peru, would be pleased with his cocktail, Lost and Found, made from Ketel One Oranje, Riesling, triple sec, and citrus, for it is served with a side order of his favourite toast and marmalade sandwiches. There are a few quirky reduced alcohol drinks, and a good list of mixed drinks, including A Less-than-Perfect Manhattan, which has the requisite rye, in this case Lot 40 Canadian rye, with Cynar artichoke amaro, fernet, maple syrup, house brine mix, and bitters. Don't miss out on the bar snacks, which are made downstairs in the Michelin-starred restaurant kitchen—who can resist duck fat chips with curry aioli or mac and cheese with shaved mushroom? The music is really varied, mainly contemporary, creating a lively buzz within the bar, without a single drop of illegal hooch in sight.

BLIND SPOT

St Martins Lane

St Martins Lane is dramatic, daring, and remarkable for its exciting interior, which features whimsical furniture designed by Phillipe Starck. The luxury hotel is fun, theatrical, and full of surprises, and Blind Spot is no exception. To find the way in, look out for the very smart façade of an old-fashioned tea counter at the back of the lobby, cast your eyes to the right, and you'll see a shiny golden hand-shaped handle, which gives you access to this innovative cocktail bar. Inside you'll find a low-lit, late-night speakeasy, designed like a modern hunting lodge and inspired by the colours and aromas of exotic tea leaves. There are mirrored alcoves and ceiling panels, intimate leather seating arrangements, comfortable club chairs, and round tables, and the bar is brought to life throughout the week with a varying programme of live music and events. You might, for example, be there celebrating National Cocktail Day or St

Patrick's Day, and you'll find inventive cocktails to reflect the occasion.

The Blind Spot drinks menu has bespoke and signature cocktails, as well as a list of classics with a twist. For example, the Bloody Andalusia is a nod at Spain, with the key ingredient, rum, in this case, Pampero Blanco, married with sherry and homemade gazpacho rather than straight tomato juice. Or try a variation on the theme of the classic Negroni, which may have begun life in Florence in 1919, but has been relocated on this menu to nearby Padua and is a seductive mix of Sipsmith gin, Luxardo bitter liqueur, Cocchi Americano, and gentian bitters. The original drink was supposedly invented when one Count Camillo Negroni marched into Florence's Caffe Casoni in 1919 and asked for a stronger version of his Americano (a mix of Campari, sweet vermouth, and soda). Apparently he had developed a taste for spirits after working as a rodeo cowboy in the American West. Thus, the Negroni was born. If you favour a Brandy Crusta, then try the refined cognac version, a perfectly balanced mix including noisette-washed Hennessy Fine de Cognac, Cherry Heering liqueur, and Jack Daniel's, plus maraschino, sugar syrup, lemon, and chocolate bitters. This is a drink with history, for the Crusta was listed by Jerry Thomas in his *Bon-Vivant's Companion* cocktail guidebook back in 1862. The bespoke cocktail list will take you on a journey around the globe and from port to port. Select from 25 destinations as you travel from New Orleans to Toledo, visiting Venice, Santorini, Beijing, and many more locations. Pair the carefully crafted drinks with nibbles from the same regions, and you can dream of being transported to exotic places by the taste and flavours.

ADDRESS:
St Martins Lane, 45 St Martin's Lane, Covent Garden, London WC2N 4HX

TEL:
+44 (0)20 7300 5588

EMAIL:
london-guestservices@sbe.com

WEB:
www.morganshotelgroup.com/originals/originals-st-martins-lane-london/eat-drink/blindspot

OPENING HOURS:
Monday to Saturday 5.00pm–1.30am (3.00am for hotel guests), Sunday 5.00pm–10.30pm (midnight for hotel guests). Food served Monday to Sunday 5.00pm–midnight.

BOOKINGS:
Via the website

AGE RESTRICTION:
21+ for the bar

EVENTS/LIVE MUSIC:
Different live music and DJs throughout the week

NEAREST UNDERGROUND STATIONS:
Leicester Square, Charing Cross

PLACES OF INTEREST NEARBY:
Trafalgar Square, National Portrait Gallery, National Gallery, Theatreland, Covent Garden

Buenos Aires, Argentina

Recipe courtesy of Blind Spot at St Martins Lane

A cocktail inspired by South America, this concoction
has a bitter, herbal, sweet taste.

INGREDIENTS

- 40ml (1¼ oz) Bacardi Oakheart spiced rum
- 25ml (¾ oz) sweet vermouth
- 10ml (2 tsp) Fernet-Branca herbal liqueur
- 10ml (2 tsp) mint syrup
- Top off with soda water
- Grapefruit slice
- Mint sprig

METHOD

Add all the liquid ingredients into a tall glass
filled with ice. Stir gently. Garnish with a
grapefruit slice and a sprig of mint.

*This recipe presents measurements for both UK and US readers. Units
are given first for UK readers in the original measurement units, then for
US readers in converted units in parentheses. Do not mix the units.*

BLUE BAR

The Berkeley

Colour-coded cocktails are the name of the game in the impeccably stylish Blue Bar, a stone's throw from Knightsbridge, Sloane Street, and Hyde Park. If you settle down in the main bar, you'll be treated to an elegant and classy room with Lutyens Blue painted walls. The colour was specially created for the hotel and pays homage to Edward Lutyens, one of the original architects of the hotel. The room is all glamour, from the dazzling white onyx bar and tabletops, mirrored wall panels, tasselled lights, and black crocodile-print leather floor to the super velvet-covered sofas and seats. If the bar is busy or you want something less traditional, then enjoy your drinks in the equally comfortable, spacious, and light glass conservatory, but wherever you are, you'll be served by cordial staff who aim to please.

Cocktails are inspired by the blue of the bar, and are grouped by colour according to their flavour: green for long and fresh, yellow for elegant and effervescent, red for rich and complex, and blue for crisp and clean. If you are a fan of tiki drinks, then try the Tiki Hopster, a rum classic brought up to date with Amaro Montenegro, passion

fruit and hops falernum, lime, and bitters. The yellow family of cocktails get their fizz from the main ingredient, Laurent-Perrier champagne, and if you prefer a non-alcoholic drink, there is an appealing selection of mocktails. The food in the Blue Bar will cure any hunger pangs, from the excellent sushi and sashimi platter, to the crispy fried tiger prawns and the Aberdeen Angus sliders with braised mushrooms, onion marmalade, and Stilton cheese. Complimentary nibbles are constantly replenished.

There is a definite wow factor here, which admittedly comes at a price, but the striking and sophisticated Blue Bar, which attracts the international set, business people, weary Knightsbridge shoppers, and everyone in between, is a very special place.

ADDRESS:
The Berkeley, Wilton Place, Knightsbridge, London SW1X 7RL

TEL:
+44 (0)20 7235 6000

EMAIL:
info@the-berkeley.co.uk

WEB:
www.the-berkeley.co.uk/restaurants-bars/blue-bar

OPENING HOURS:
Monday to Saturday 12.00pm–1.00am, Sunday 12.00pm–11.00pm

BOOKINGS:
Not taken

DRESS CODE:
Elegant smart casual; no shorts, vests, sportswear, flip-flops, ripped jeans, or baseball caps

AGE RESTRICTION:
18+

NEAREST UNDERGROUND STATIONS:
Knightsbridge, Hyde Park Corner

PLACES OF INTEREST NEARBY:
Harvey Nichols, Harrods, Hyde Park, Green Park, Sloane Street and Knightsbridge designer shopping, Natural History Museum, Science Museum, Royal Albert Hall

BOURNE & HOLLINGSWORTH BUILDINGS

B ourne & Hollingsworth Buildings is a great place to chill out, with multiple alternative rooms to relax in. You can perch yourself at the marble mosaic bar itself and engage with the friendly mixologists, or there is a homey, comfy lounge area with a feeling of faded grandeur about it where you can relax and generally unwind, taking in views of the leafy park beyond. For the ultimate cocktail experience, there is Below and Hidden Club, an intimate basement drinking and dancing den no bigger than an average living room. The space undergoes a transformation at nighttime, when light panels illuminate the tapestry-covered walls and the DJ gets going.

Wherever you find yourself within B&H Buildings, the cocktail list is bound to please, for B&H hallmark cocktails feature classics and ever-changing seasonal creations. Of course, you can also order anything that takes your fancy. A feature on the summertime menu might be the Kentucky Derby favourite, Georgia Mint Julep, a

ADDRESS:
42 Northampton Road, Clerkenwell,
London EC1R 0HU

TEL:
+44 (0)20 3174 1156

EMAIL:
info@bandhbuildings.com

WEB:
www.bandhbuildings.com/
bh-buildings

OPENING HOURS:
Monday to Thursday 11.00am–
midnight, Friday 11.00am–1.00am,
Saturday 10.00am–1.00am,
Sunday 10.00am–6.00pm

BOOKINGS:
Reservation team available from
9.00am–6.00pm by phone; you can
also book via the website

AGE RESTRICTION:
18+ after 7.00pm

**NEAREST UNDERGROUND
STATIONS:**
Farringdon, Angel

**PLACES OF
INTEREST NEARBY:**
Clerkenwell, Exmouth Market,
Sadler's Wells Theatre, London
Metropolitan Archives

thirst-quenching ice cold blend of Wild Turkey
rye whiskey, Merlet cognac, Lejay crème de
pêche, and fresh mint. There's a playful version
of the modern classic cosmopolitan, made
of Wyborowa vodka, Merlet Trois Citrus
liqueur, fresh lime, and cranberry juice. Or try
the bold and boozy take on a Mai Tai, mixed
from Appleton Signature Blend and Wray
and Nephew Jamaican rums, Pierre Ferrand
dry curaçao, fresh lime, and orgeat. Brilliant
bar bites from veggie fritters to a beefburger
are bound to satisfy. If you are eating here as
well, then there is the café, the garden room,
the greenhouse, and a private dining room.
On weekends there are special cocktails that
complement the yummy brunch comfort food.
What better reason can there be to visit?

BRUMUS BAR

Haymarket Hotel

Don't be deceived by the traditional exterior of the Haymarket Hotel, for inside it is chic and cosmopolitan. It's an adventure, and the interior décor will make you smile. Just take a look at the back of the quirky bar seats, which are appliqued with your favourite pooches: poodles, Scottie dogs, dachshunds, and more. Fabric-covered columns, Indian artwork, comfortable seating, and low background music make for the perfect place for a pre-theatre cocktail. You couldn't do better, for Brumus Bar is in the heart of London's Theatreland, right next door to the famous Haymarket Theatre Royal.

The seemingly endless drinks list includes a great signature menu: cricket and gin lovers might try Silly Mid Wicket, a fruity mix of Bombay Sapphire gin with rhubarb liqueur, pink grapefruit, and basil. Amongst the revisited classics, a winter version of the traditional cosmopolitan mixes Ketel One Oranje, warming Cointreau and ginger, and carrot juice—not guaranteed to help your night vision. Another classic you

ADDRESS:
Haymarket Hotel, 1 Suffolk Place,
St James's, London SW1Y 4HX

TEL:
+44 (0)20 7470 4007

EMAIL:
brumus@haymarkethotel.com

WEB:
www.firmdalehotels.com/a/
restaurants-bars/london/brumus

OPENING HOURS:
Monday to Saturday
11.00am–11.30pm, Sunday and
public holidays 11.00am–10.30pm.
Extended hours for hotel guests.

BOOKINGS:
By phone or online

AGE RESTRICTION:
18+

**NEAREST UNDERGROUND
STATIONS:**
Piccadilly Circus

**PLACES OF
INTEREST NEARBY:**
Regent Street and Jermyn Street
shopping, Trafalgar Square, National
Gallery, National Portrait Gallery,
St James's Park

might find on the list is Brumus's own take on
the Sazerac, where cinnamon infused Rémy
Martin VSOP is paired with Rittenhouse
Bottled-in-Bond rye whiskey, giving the taste
buds a sweet kick. A short but bubbly list of
sparkling cocktails includes the Pear Drop
Bellini, which uses the bar's own pear drop
syrup shaken with Grey Goose La Poire vodka,
fresh lemon juice, and Prosecco. And whilst
you are sipping your personal tipple, have a bite
to eat. The bar menu offers a good selection
of tasty tapas and sandwiches, including a
Croque Monsieur, the Haymarket club, and
the Brumus burger, as well as more substantial
platters. One thing is for sure: you won't
go hungry.

CAHOOTS

If you fancy having a really jolly time enjoying excellent cocktails in a very unusual setting, then definitely head for Cahoots. You'll find it tucked away in a passage off the central part of Kingly Court, Soho, with the black entrance door guarded by a friendly minder. The fun begins here whilst you wait for him to check your booking before you head downstairs into the converted, disused underground station. On arrival, you will find yourself transported back to post-war Britain, seated in look-alike underground train carriages and surrounded by late 1940s posters and memorabilia. The Captain and his team of 'scoundrels' are happy to advise you on cocktails from the huge list, all set out in the four-page newspaper, *The Kingly Court Herald*. You get to choose from classic cocktails and post-war favourites, all served up in a variety of 1940s memorabilia, from enamelled mugs to hip flasks, vintage milk bottles and tins,

ADDRESS:
13 Kingly Court, Soho, London
W1B 5PW

TEL:
+44 (0)20 7352 6200

EMAIL:
highspirits@cahoots-london.com

WEB:
www.cahoots-london.com

OPENING HOURS:
Monday to Wednesday
5.00pm–2.00am, Thursday
5.00pm–3.00am, Friday
4.00pm–3.00am, Saturday
1.00pm–3.00am, Sunday
3.00pm–midnight

BOOKINGS:
Advised; via the website

DRESS CODE:
1940s dress very welcome. No
sportswear or casual footwear.

AGE RESTRICTION:
21+

EVENTS/LIVE MUSIC:
Varied; see description

**NEAREST UNDERGROUND
STATIONS:**
Oxford Circus

**PLACES OF
INTEREST NEARBY:**
BBC Broadcasting House, Carnaby
Street, Liberty London, Hamleys,
Regent Street, Chinatown, Piccadilly,
Trocadero Entertainment Centre

and mismatched teacups. Collections range from 'Easy Drinking', 'Elegant', 'Loaded and Punchy', 'Classy', 'Home-Made', 'Cahooch', 'Virgin', and 'Creamy'—how about trying A Lovely Bunch of Coconuts? Sharing cocktails are a hoot: ten pals can share a number called Meet Me Under the Station Clock, concocted from gin, cherry liqueur, lemon, apple juice, mint, and cucumber, all topped up with a full bottle of Moët & Chandon champagne. And believe it or not, it's served up in a station clock.

Feeling hungry? Then take your pick from the list of good, old-fashioned rations on offer. Toasties (melt sandwiches) include a cheese and, love it or hate it, Marmite offering, and a selection of platform pastries—savory pies to you and me—are all served up in old tins.

If you linger into the late evening any night from Wednesday to Sunday, then you'll be able to enjoy live music, which ranges from jazz to swing, rock 'n' roll, and beyond. Vintage records are played from inside a recycled piano, and you can join in with a sing-a-long and a knees-up, song sheets provided. On a Thursday, Friday, or Saturday, you can join in the fun and dance the night away. Cahoots is a really good themed bar that charms and impresses from the beginning, and it's lively enough for a party of friends to have a ball. As Cahoots would say, 'Bottoms up, folks!'

CALLOOH CALLAY

There is never a dull moment at Callooh Callay, a neighbourhood bar in Shoreditch not far from busy Old Street. It's as eccentric as its name, which were words chortled by Lewis Carroll's imaginary creature, the Jabberwock. And it's not for the faint-hearted, as the main front bar is buzzing with retro 70s and 80s music. There's a lot of exposed brick and old timbers, retro chairs, mirrors, and upholstered stools. You'll find the menu inside an empty cassette case, and if you need the loo, that's hidden behind a wardrobe door. The same door takes you to a hallway and a pair of plush curtains; go through these, and you'll find the back lounge, a bigger, bookable space with full-on retro-disco styling and the quirkiest of seats, including a reclaimed roll top bath cut in half to create two small sofas, with plenty of cushions to make it comfortable.

ADDRESS:
65 Rivington Street, Shoreditch,
London EC2A 3AY

TEL:
+44 (0)20 7739 4781

EMAIL:
freyja@calloohcallaybar.com

WEB:
www.calloohcallaybar.com

OPENING HOURS:
Daily 6.00pm–1.00am

BOOKINGS:
Via the website or email. Maximum
table reservations in the back lounge
for up to eight guests.

AGE RESTRICTION:
21+

MASTERCLASSES:
Details on the website

**NEAREST UNDERGROUND
STATIONS:**
Old Street

**PLACES OF
INTEREST NEARBY:**
XOYO, Wesley's Chapel and
Museum of Methodism, Bunhill
Fields

Both areas have the same menu, and you'll find a helpful description of each cocktail on it, many of them including interesting and unusual ingredients. There is green sorrel in the gin-based Oma Forest, and a real kick from the Guajillo chilli in Roselle. Or how about the dark chocolate, cola, and orange juice in the Bulleit bourbon–based Fontana? Tucked away at the very back of the hallway are the stairs to JubJub, an intimate members-only bar (no charge to join), excellent for small groups, and where the bartenders take turns each week to create a bespoke menu. An added attraction are the group cocktail masterclasses—for 6–20 people—where you get hands-on instruction in recreating the bar's drinks. There's a really convivial atmosphere at Callooh Callay, with something for everyone, and it's a super place to let your hair down.

CLARIDGE'S BAR

Claridge's

Claridge's Bar has a justifiable reputation as a world-class venue and does not disappoint. The legendary hotel has hosted a list of illustrious visitors from Queen Victoria to Winston Churchill and Audrey Hepburn to Cary Grant, and is a sophisticated rendezvous. True to the 1920s refurbishment, the interior of Claridge's Bar is most definitely Art Deco influenced, all glamour and glitz. Champagne lovers have an array of cocktails to choose from, and can indulge in the likes of the All the Year Round, named after Charles Dickens' 1892 work. The main ingredient was falernum, to which Claridge's have added pisco, fresh pineapple, lemon, and Laurent-Perrier Brut. Another, The Flapper, was created when the bar first opened, and you can still enjoy the delicious combination of strawberries, crème de cassis, and Laurent-Perrier. If you choose from the 'Claridge's Cocktails' list, you are sure to be impressed. Take Treat for Kings, which serves as a reminder of how pineapples were once so expensive that only royalty could afford them, and there was no better way

to demonstrate your wealth than by serving one to your guests. Now all you have to do is enjoy this wonderful cocktail, which blends Ilegal mezcal with agave and, of course, fresh pineapple. There is also a unique twist on the classic martini in Brook Street, which has Jensen's Old Tom gin and the addition of Carpano Antica Formula and a dash of citrus.

The cocktails are crafted with care and the staff are courteous, considerate, and make you feel like a million dollars. As you would expect, the bar food menu is exceptional, ranging from caviar, oysters, and sushi to a Caesar salad and a rather super sandwich. The bar can get very busy, and you can't make reservations, but it is a real top-notch treat and well worth the effort and price tag.

ADDRESS:
Claridge's, Brook Street, Mayfair, London W1K 4HR

TEL:
+44 (0)20 7629 8860

EMAIL:
info@claridges.co.uk

WEB:
www.claridges.co.uk/restaurants-bars/claridges-bar

OPENING HOURS:
Monday to Saturday 12.00pm–1.00am, Sunday 12.00pm–midnight

BOOKINGS:
Not taken

DRESS CODE:
Smart casual

AGE RESTRICTION:
18+ after 6.00pm, but prior to that children who are staying as guests at the hotel are welcome with adult supervision

NEAREST UNDERGROUND STATIONS:
Bond Street

PLACES OF INTEREST NEARBY:
The Wallace Collection, Bond Street, Regent Street, Green Park, Hyde Park

CONNAUGHT BAR

The Connaught

The mixologists at the Connaught Bar are as equally skilled at preparing time-honoured legendary cocktails as they are at inventing new creations, making this luxe bar an ideal venue for everyone. The surroundings are sleek, evocative of 1920s English and Irish Cubist art. In the daytime it's light and airy, and the cool grey décor adds a calm stylishness. The exceptionally comfortable leather seating arrangements provide intimate spaces. At night, the platinum silver leaf on the textured wall panels shines and shimmers, and the tables are candlelit, adding a magical quality.

If you are a martini fan, then you get the full treatment here, with the martini trolley brought to your table. Under the guidance of your mixologist, you get to choose your own bitters before the drink is created for you with a good degree of theatricality. The bar is renowned for its legendary cocktails, and the 'Masterpieces' list includes very many well-known recipes that have been redesigned and given a new, modern twist. Fleurissimo, a tribute to a former guest, Princess Grace of Monaco, is

ADDRESS:
The Connaught, Carlos Place,
Mayfair, London W1K 2AL

TEL:
+44 (0)20 7314 3419

EMAIL:
info@the-connaught.co.uk

WEB:
www.the-connaught.co.uk/
restaurants-bars/connaught-bar

OPENING HOURS:
Monday to Saturday
11.00am–1.00am, Sunday
11.00am–midnight

BOOKINGS:
Not taken

DRESS CODE:
Smart casual

AGE RESTRICTION:
18+ after 6.00pm

MASTERCLASSES:
Master the Mix, limited to 6 people.
Call +44 (0)20 3147 7103 or email
arobakova@the-connaught.co.uk.

**NEAREST UNDERGROUND
STATIONS:**
Bond Street, Green Park

**PLACES OF
INTEREST NEARBY:**
Mayfair, Balenciaga and Marc Jacobs
flagship stores, Gagosian Gallery,
Dunhill's Bourdon House, Bond
Street, Marylebone High Street

an updated version of a champagne cocktail, which comes from the mix of Rémy Martin cognac, homemade Connaught bitters, violet liqueur, a sugar cube, and Laurent-Perrier champagne. Another drink is a reinvention of the 1931 Fanciulli recipe from the Waldorf Astoria cocktail book. It's the cardamom leaf infused Woodford Reserve whiskey and black cardamom syrup that update it, a change from Fernet-Branca. The new collection of carefully constructed cocktails, 'The Essence', takes its inspiration from the architecture, the guests, the atmosphere, and the imaginative ingredients. You'll find creative drinks, including non-alcoholic offerings, grouped as 'Foundation', 'Finesse', and 'Flair', all a tribute to the skill of the mixologists. Being presented with the recipe card of your favourite cocktail when you leave is an unexpected treat. Plus, the bar menu has delicious food guaranteed to tempt the taste buds, from canapés and caviar to less extravagant small bites and delectable desserts. A very beautiful bar indeed.

DONOVAN BAR

Brown's Hotel

Y ou can reach the Donovan Bar either from inside Brown's Hotel or from the dedicated entrance on Albemarle Street. It's a glamorous and sophisticated space, cool on a hot day and warm on a chilly evening, and the interior is striking, from the ultra-sleek bronze-topped bar to the original 19th-century stained glass window. Sitting amidst some of the most iconic black and white photographs taken by the bar's namesake, Sir Terence Donovan, you'll be very comfortably seated at the bar if there is room, or at a sculpted glass-top table. There is even a 'naughty corner', which offers an intimate, semi-private bookable area for up to 12 people. And to keep up with the naughtiness, you can order a spiced-up, fruity, rum-based cocktail of the same name.

The most admired fashion photographer of the 1960s, Donovan has inspired Salvatore Calabrese's unique cocktail menu. The celebrated drinks maestro not only honors forgotten and best-loved classics, but has also created signature and vintage

ADDRESS:
Brown's Hotel, 33 Albemarle Street,
Mayfair, London W1S 4BP

TEL: +44 (0)20 7493 6020

EMAIL: thedonovanbar@
roccofortehotels.com

WEB: www.roccofortehotels.com/
hotels-and-resorts/browns-hotel/
restaurants-and-bars/donovan-bar

OPENING HOURS:
Monday to Saturday 11.00am–
1.00am, Sunday and public holidays
11.00am–midnight

BOOKINGS:
Not taken except for larger groups
wishing to book the Naughty Corner

DRESS CODE: Smart casual;
trainers/sneakers, T-shirts, shorts,
and sportswear are not permitted

AGE RESTRICTION:
18+ after 5.00pm. Children are
allowed during the day accompanied
by an adult.

EVENTS/LIVE MUSIC:
Live jazz on Thursday, Friday, and
Saturday nights

**NEAREST UNDERGROUND
STATIONS:**
Piccadilly Circus, Green Park

**PLACES OF INTEREST
NEARBY:** Royal Academy of Arts,
Burlington Arcade, Green Park,
St James's Park, Bond Street, Cork
Street art galleries, Savile Row,
Fortnum & Mason

recipes. If you want to push the boat out, then besides the caviar, you can indulge in a Vesper, the bespoke cocktail that James Bond ordered in *Casino Royale*, famously shaken but not stirred. Calabrese sticks to Bond's ingredients but uses vintage spirits of the day: Gordon's gin circa 1950, Smirnoff vodka circa 1950, and the all-important Kina Lillet 1949, the original aromatized wine with quinine, which, apart from being used elsewhere for medicinal purposes, gives the drink its individuality. Signature cocktails are listed to help you choose a mix to match your mood. 'High Exposure' are bright and refreshing drinks, whilst dark and mellow flavours are captured in 'Low Exposure'. Strong and bold ingredients are featured in 'High Contrast', and soft and delicate drinks are grouped under 'Low Contrast'. Order some bar food if you are feeling peckish, from caviar to more humble snacks, larger plates, and desserts. The Donovan Bar is altogether a lovely place, intimate enough for a date, with really good cocktails and a smooth mood on Thursday, Friday, and Saturday nights when live jazz is on the menu.

EXPERIMENTAL COCKTAIL CLUB

Here is a clue to finding the secret and hidden Experimental Cocktail Club, which has no number or name on the door. It's almost opposite 36 Gerrard Street, and has a shabby chic, peeling painted door that you can easily miss. Don't be tempted to give up and go home. But rather than standing on the street whilst you wait for a table, make sure you book in advance. Once the unassuming doorman holding fort outside with his clipboard has let you in, you'll be escorted upstairs to the cosy bar, the London outpost of the French original. You can't miss the Parisian bijou charm of the place, with exposed brickwork, luxurious velvet upholstered seating, and mirrored walls and ceilings. When the curtains are drawn, it's like being in a private house, but with a bar. Spreading upward over two floors of a townhouse with regular live music floating through the rooms, the bar has a speakeasy feel about it.

The experimental bit doesn't stretch to test tubes; rather, the mixologists have created carefully crafted and unusual combinations that do change with the seasons. If you like

ADDRESS:
13A Gerrard Street, Chinatown,
London W1D 5PS

TEL:
None; bookings via email only

EMAIL:
reservations@chinatownecc.com

WEB:
www.chinatownecc.com

OPENING HOURS:
Monday to Saturday 6.00pm–
3.00am, Sunday 6.00pm–midnight.
£5 cover charge after 11.00pm.

BOOKINGS:
Not essential; walk-ins are first come,
first served. Bookings via email only.
Reservations desk is open Monday to
Saturday until 5.00pm.

AGE RESTRICTION:
18+

**NEAREST UNDERGROUND
STATIONS:**
Leicester Square

**PLACES OF
INTEREST NEARBY:**
Chinatown, Piccadilly, Leicester
Square, Theatreland

a milky punch, then try the rather exotic, and perennial favourite, Kota Ternate. It's a twist on a piña colada, but is lighter—they use clarified milk rather than cream—and very fruity, spiced, and complex, with its own unique taste. It's even served in a medicine bottle so you can pour out your own 'dose'. If you are a martini fan, then try Double O Pandan for an about-turn—there's no James Bond here. This twist on the original uses more vermouth, and the vodka is infused with pandan leaf, which is originally from Indonesia. The result is a rich and very particular flavour, both buttery and herbal. The coffee gives a kick to the drink, and on top of all that, it's low ABV.

A small but tasty bar snack menu has excellent charcuterie, soda bread, cheese, and more, all good for sharing. There's a great recipe book named after the bar for you to buy, so you can be your own mixologist. By following the basic step-by-step instructions, you can create some of the ECC classics as well as a selection of the lesser-known cocktails. But it's no substitute for visiting this cool bar, which has flair and style; and with a 3.00am licence Monday to Saturday, you can drink to your heart's, and pockets', content.

THE FUMOIR

Claridge's

Those in the know have been enjoying cocktails in the discreet Fumoir since 1929, when it was, as the name suggests, a smoking lounge. Of the two bars at Claridge's, this is the quietest and most intimate, and you'll find it tucked away in the Art Deco interior. It's recognisable by the René Lalique glass panel bearing the name above the door, and is gloriously glamorous. The décor is deep purple and the walls are inset with Lalique glass panels and hung with William Klein's unconventional portraits. Added to all this, the seating is oh so comfortable, upholstered in plush ruby-red velvet. The

horseshoe-shaped bar, topped with a slab of black marble, sets the stage for the mixologists to work their magic, which is of course the reason for your visit.

The bar will not disappoint. Classic cocktails, like the mint julep, have been redesigned to suit the modern palate without losing sight of their origins. Claridge's Signature Julep has the bourbon, of course—Adrien Camut 6 Year Old calvados—along with the bar's own raspberry preserve, fresh mint, and Laurent-Perrier La Cuvée, and is ideal as a pre-theatre long drink. If mezcal is your tipple, then try Maguey, served short and created from Ilegal mezcal, Ardbeg whisky, absinthe, raspberries, and citrus. There's a good list of specific champagne and temperance cocktails, and the bar food is exceptional. At the end of the day, why not relax with a vodka martini, brought to you in an ice-cold glass?

ADDRESS:
Claridge's, Brook Street, Mayfair, London W1A 2JQ

TEL:
+44 (0)20 7629 8860

EMAIL:
info@claridges.co.uk

WEB:
www.claridges.co.uk/restaurants-bars/the-fumoir

OPENING HOURS:
Monday to Saturday
12.00pm–1.00am,
Sunday 12.00pm–midnight

BOOKINGS:
Not taken

AGE RESTRICTION:
18+ except children who are hotel guests, who many enter until 6.00pm and must be accompanied by an adult

NEAREST UNDERGROUND STATIONS:
Bond Street

PLACES OF INTEREST NEARBY:
The Wallace Collection, Bond Street, Regent Street, Green Park, Hyde Park

THE GLADE

Nothing at sketch is conventional, least of all the Glade, so prepare yourself for a journey into an ethereal fairyland where rays of light beam down on you. The walls of this woodland bar are decorated with hand-cut découpage leaves, flowers, and forest trees, and the lush carpet is sculpted to resemble pine needles and grass. The upholstery is all vibrant jewel-coloured velvet, the dainty tables have tinted mirror tops, and the background music comes from a transparent pink self-playing piano. But remember that you are here for the excellent drinks as well as the idiosyncratic atmosphere! The menu is a work of art in itself. Classics, some with a twist, include Cosmo Royal, a bubbly version of a cosmopolitan, and there is a sweet, fruity, and

ADDRESS:
sketch, 9 Conduit Street, Mayfair,
London W1S 2XG

TEL:
+44 (0)20 7659 4500

EMAIL:
info@sketch.london

WEB:
www.sketch.london/the-glade

OPENING HOURS:
Monday to Saturday 5.00pm–
2.00am, Sunday 5.00pm–12.30am.
Bar snacks served 5.00pm–10.00pm.

BOOKINGS:
Not taken

DRESS CODE:
'Art Smart'; please dress with a sense
of style and character. No beachwear
or sportswear.

AGE RESTRICTION:
18+

**NEAREST UNDERGROUND
STATIONS:**
Oxford Circus, Bond Street,
Piccadilly Circus

**PLACES OF
INTEREST NEARBY:**
Bond Street, Regent Street, Royal
Academy, Oxford Street

refreshing Russian Spring Punch, described by
the 1980s creator Dick Bradsell as basically a
spiked Kir Royal over ice. Served in a highball,
the fizz here comes from Prosecco. You also
have a list of 'Parlour Editions' and 'Virgin
Libations' to choose from. On the first list, look
out for the indulgent Banana Daiquiri. As
you can guess, it's loaded with banana and is
concocted from Zacapa 23, falernum, banana

liqueur, banana sherbet, coconut cream, and Angostura bitters, and it's served in a coupette. And don't forget the food, which is as imaginative as the cocktails, from savoury mini tartlets to assorted tempura and aubergine caviar. An unforgettable place.

Other sketch bars (all at the same address) include the Parlour and the East Bar. The Parlour is transformed at night into a neon-lit, vibrant cocktail lounge. The resident DJ is in charge of the diverse entertainment and you can dance the night away whilst enjoying the signature cocktails and being reminded of early 1990s decadence. The East Bar is white, bright, and like a giant spaceship; it's a real evening bar for unusual as well as a few classic cocktails. Walk-ins only.

GREEN BAR

Hotel Café Royal

If the Green Bar is not too busy when you arrive, do sit at the semi-circular steel bar—you can move to a table later if you like—and let the bartenders help you decide on the right cocktail to match your mood, or mix up your favoured drink. The welcoming staff are more than delighted to share their expertise and knowledge with you and, whilst you decide, to bring you complimentary nibbles and a drink of rum, lime, cherry liqueur, and sloe gin, accompanied by a glass of water. The bar is intimate and cosy, with club chairs and leather banquette seating, and the music is at just the right level to not drown out conversation. There is an enviable cocktail-making heritage here, and many of the drinks are inspired by the 1937 *Café Royal Cocktail Book*. Take Picador, for example, better known as a margarita today, which combines

ADDRESS:
Hotel Café Royal, 15 Glasshouse
Street, Soho, London W1B 4DY

TEL:
+44 (0)20 7406 3310

EMAIL:
restaurants@hotelcaferoyal.com

WEB:
www.hotelcaferoyal.com/greenbar

OPENING HOURS:
Daily 12.00pm–midnight

BOOKINGS:
Not taken

DRESS CODE:
Smart casual

AGE RESTRICTION:
18+

**NEAREST UNDERGROUND
STATIONS:**
Piccadilly Circus

**PLACES OF
INTEREST NEARBY:**
Theatreland, Soho, Regent Street,
Trafalgar Square, Piccadilly,
Trocadero Entertainment Centre

tequila with tangy lime juice and the zesty
orange of Cointreau. The Green Bar makes
the most of London's long history of using
botanicals in gin production and mixology,
with carefully crafted signature cocktails that
celebrate the individual character of each
gin, with the perfect garnish to complete
the experience.

The gin journey includes Portobello Road
No. 171, a handcrafted gin with nine botanical
ingredients from around the world, served with
Fever Tree Indian tonic, orange, and rosemary.
The eponymous Dodd's uses the small-batch

organic gin named after the enterprising Ralph Dodd, who tried to set up a distillery in London in the 1800s, and combines it with the delicate and floral Fever Tree Mediterranean tonic, fresh chillies, and lemon peel.

This bar is also a place where the absinthe culture, so beloved of the late 19th-century Bohemian set, including Oscar Wilde, who frequented the hotel, has been revitalised. The vibrant green drink, or 'Green Fairy', once banned because of its addictive and hallucinogenic qualities, is served through the traditional absinthe bar-top fountains, and cocktails are created that entice and challenge common taste conceptions.

The Green Bar offers skinny cocktails, mocktails that use the innovative non-alcoholic spirit Seedlip, hot cocktails, seasonal cocktails, and a small bar snacks menu. Whether you are a visitor to the capital city or a native Londoner, you'll find yourself drinking in a brilliant, beautiful bar.

HAM YARD BAR

Ham Yard Hotel

Ham Yard Bar is almost always busy and buzzing and is very much the 'in' place. The décor is bold, bright, and eclectic, and the place has a private club feel about it, making it just the place for a pre-theatre or post-shopping cocktail, to say nothing of an after-work unwinder or just because you fancy an excellent tipple. Arrive early to get a seat at the long pewter bar or get comfy on one of the orange leather banquettes.

The cocktail menu here is broken down into categories with list changes in spring and winter, with new mixes reflecting the season. Expect fresher, crisper, fruitier cocktails through spring and summer, and more complex drinks for the colder months. Then there are sparkling, tailor-made martinis using vodka or gin. Amongst the perennial favourites is the Ham Yard Gin and Tonic, a twist between a Negroni and a gin and tonic. Made with Portobello Road gin, there's a lovely balance between the freshness of the grapefruit bitters, St-Germain elderflower liqueur, and homemade

grapefruit tonic water versus the bitterness of the Campari. Or, if you like a margarita, then go for a Black Margarita. The blackberry purée makes it fruitier than usual, but this burst of fruit is balanced out by a subtle kick and the lovely herbal character of the thyme fat-washed Herradura Plata. The addition of lime, agave, and a rim-rolled black salt makes for a super drink. And then there is the bar food, with anything from olives and spiced mixed nuts to delicious small and large plates as well as desserts. You may find it hard to resist a truffle mac and cheese melt, or a platter of Loch Fyne smoked salmon with sourdough toast, and even harder to say no to a decadent chocolate liégeois.

ADDRESS:
Ham Yard Hotel, 1 Ham Yard, Soho, London W1D 7DT

TEL:
+44 (0)20 3642 1007

EMAIL:
restaurant@hamyardhotel.com

WEB:
www.firmdalehotels.com/a/restaurants-bars/london/ham-yard

OPENING HOURS:
Monday to Saturday 11.00am–11.30pm, Sunday and public holidays 11.00am–10.30pm. Extended hours for hotel guests.

BOOKINGS:
Not taken, but the space can be booked for large parties

AGE RESTRICTION:
18+

NEAREST UNDERGROUND STATIONS:
Piccadilly Circus

PLACES OF INTEREST NEARBY:
Theatreland, Soho, Regent Street, Trafalgar Square, Piccadilly, Leicester Square

HARVEY NICHOLS
FIFTH FLOOR BAR

Speed straight up to the fifth floor of Harvey Nichols—the lift is inside the lobby of the entrance at the corner of Sloane Street and Knightsbridge—and take the mirrored passage into the stunning bar that gives you a view of the Knightsbridge skyline. It's an equally perfect venue for a pit stop from your retail therapy, an end-of-the-day relaxing drink, a date with friends, or a celebration. The newly created décor is sophisticated and timeless, with a color scheme of earthy tones and subtle shades of pinks and greys, humorous tasseled lampshades, soft and curvy suede sofas, and plush chairs, all offset against metallic and steel furnishings. The music shifts from discreet to toe-tapping as the evening progresses, really enlivening the place.

The mixologists have created an inventive cocktail list that takes its inspiration from the various areas of London. Just take a look at the 'East London' drinks influenced by the area's edgy, hipster feel and sense of movement—Midas Touch features Ketel One vodka, lightly citrus Italicus, mastika, and Noilly Prat with Pierre Ferrand curaçao. In 'South London', you'll find drinks which take into account the

ADDRESS:
109–125 Knightsbridge, Belgravia,
London SW1X 7RJ

TEL: +44 (0)20 7235 5250

EMAIL:
reception@harveynichols.com

WEB: www.harveynichols.com/
restaurant/knightsbridge-dining/bar

OPENING HOURS:
Monday to Thursday 12.00pm–
11.00pm, Friday 12.00pm–midnight,
Saturday 12:30pm–midnight, Sunday
12.00pm–8.00pm

BOOKINGS: Via phone or email;
walk-ins welcome

AGE RESTRICTION:
None, but those under 18 need to be
seated at a table rather than at the bar

MASTERCLASSES:
Group classes run on Saturday
and Sunday mornings from
10.00am–12.00pm, followed by lunch
at the Fifth Floor Café. Contact via
email.

**NEAREST UNDERGROUND
STATIONS:** Knightsbridge

**PLACES OF
INTEREST NEARBY:**
Harvey Nichols, Harrods, Hyde
Park, Green Park, Sloane Street and
Knightsbridge designer shopping,
Natural History Museum, Science
Museum, Royal Albert Hall

nearby docks and the diversity of the local population, exemplified by Prime Meridian, a mix of pear eau de vie, mastika, white chocolate, and thyme. If you are feeling virtuous, or just more aware of your health, body, and lifestyle, then the non-alcoholic cocktails include No One Knows, an alcohol-free Bellini, and the No-jito, an alcohol-free mojito. On the classic side, the espresso martini is a sophisticated and sumptuous mix of vodka, coffee liqueur, and espresso, with a hint of vanilla. In fact, overall you'll find a cocktail list where seasonal ingredients and first-class spirits from all over the world are of prime importance. And the food is also rather good, from bar snacks to classics, including a Caesar salad and a chicken club sandwich to fish and chips and yummy desserts. Harvey Nichols has always had a reputation for being chic, and the Fifth Floor Bar certainly comes up to expectations.

LADIES & GENTLEMEN

The essence of a secret bar is, of course, the location, and nowhere gets much more surprising than this chilled-out neighbourhood venue, housed in what was a Victorian public convenience (bathroom). You'll find it in the middle of a busy junction very close to Kentish Town tube station. Make your way down the stairs from the street, push back the velvet curtain over the doorway, and you are in the small, intimate, and cosy bar, where it's table service in the two small rooms. If you prefer, grab a stool at the centrepiece bar. There are bookshelves and vintage speakers, the original wall tiles are still there, and there is the odd cistern hanging on the wall to remind you of the venue's earlier life as a public loo. It's a really good place for a pre-dinner cocktail, or, if you have been at the O2 Forum—another recycled building, this time from a huge cinema—then just cross the road for a post-gig tipple.

ADDRESS:
2 Highgate Road, Highgate, London
NW5 1NR (on corner with Fortress
Road and Kentish Town Road)

TEL:
+44 (0)20 7813 7562

EMAIL:
attendant@ladiesandgents.co

WEB:
www.ladiesandgents.co

OPENING HOURS:
Sunday to Thursday 7.00pm–
midnight, Friday and Saturday
5.00pm–late

BOOKINGS:
Advisable, via the website, email, or
telephone

AGE RESTRICTION:
18+

**NEAREST UNDERGROUND
STATIONS:**
Kentish Town

**PLACES OF
INTEREST NEARBY:**
Camden Market, O2 Forum, Kentish
Town City Farm

Seasonal cocktails use fresh produce collected from allotments around nearby Hampstead Heath, and the menu changes twice a year. There is a 16-litre (4-gallon) micro distillery that produces in-house gin and low-alcohol spirits for the cocktails. Whether you like your martini wet or dry, with an olive or a twist of lemon peel, then the Vestal 5oz Martini is for you, made from Polish Vestal craft potato vodka, dry vermouth, and ice. Shaken or stirred? It really depends on whether you follow James Bond. Ladies & Gentlemen is certainly not a bog-standard venue, and is a really cosy, welcoming bar that's worth seeking out.

LITTLE BAT

This is a real neighbourhood bar where you can enjoy cocktails with your brunch from 10.00 in the morning until 4.00 in the afternoon and then move on to the main cocktail menu and great bar food and sharing platters. Straight off the street, there is a touch of Alice in Wonderland here. From the summery feeling in the front as you walk further into this cosy, welcoming bar, you'll find a long room resembling a library, a bar with plenty of seating, and beyond, as the light recedes, more intimate spaces with deep armchairs and semi-circular banquettes in jade leather. The cocktail list, which includes seasonal changes, is extensive, and the friendly staff are delighted to offer advice. Choose from light and refreshing, tropical, citrussy, fruity, stirred down

ADDRESS:
54 Islington Park Street, Islington,
London N1 1PX

TEL:
+44 (0)20 7359 6070

EMAIL:
hello@litttlebatbar.com

WEB:
www.littlebatbar.com

OPENING HOURS:
Tuesday and Wednesday
10.00am–11.00pm, Thursday
10.00am–midnight, Friday and
Saturday 10.00am–1.00am, Sunday
10.00am–6.00pm. Closed Monday.

BOOKINGS:
Via email

AGE RESTRICTION:
21+

**NEAREST UNDERGROUND
STATIONS:**
Highbury & Islington

**PLACES OF
INTEREST NEARBY:**
Emirates Stadium, Highbury Fields,
Almeida Theatre

and brown—imagine the Biscuit Old fashioned, made from bourbon, biscuit syrup, and Aztec chocolate bitters—or after dinner, which could include Little Bat's own Ourspresso Martini. Even when the menu is seasonally updated, the mixologists always retain the most popular mixes, including the perennially popular Driving Miss Daisy, an alcohol-free mix of Seedlip Spice 94, apple shrub, Angostura bitters, citrus, and soda. Add gin for a boozy version. If you are a regular visitor here, then take a look at the family cabinet system. You can leave a bottle of your favourite spirit on the top shelf behind the bar, drink from it for free, and if anyone else wants a tipple, you get money off your next bill. A win-win situation. Little Bat suits a cosy date night, a weekend celebration, or a pre- or post-theatre drink as well as a casual cocktail after work.

THE LOBBY BAR

One Aldwych

The glamorous Lobby Bar within One Aldwych is just a stone's throw from Covent Garden and Theatreland. If you need an excuse to visit, it is the most perfect place to celebrate, enjoy a pre- or post-theatre cocktail, meet for a date, or simply catch up with friends and colleagues. The Edwardian hotel building is, to say the least, impressive, and has an illustrious past as home to the *Morning Post* newspaper, the Ministry of Defence, and Lloyds Bank, amongst others.

There are two cocktail menus to select from, including a 'Lobby Bar Classics' list, with knowledgeable mixologists and staff on hand to give you the heads-up on what to choose. A second list of imaginative creations is worth sampling—for example, the recent 'Showtime Cocktails' list, which changes seasonally, has been created by

ADDRESS:
One Aldwych, 1 Aldwych, Covent
Garden, London WC2B 4BZ

TEL:
+44 (0)20 7300 1070

EMAIL:
lobbybar@onealdwych.com

WEB:
www.onealdwych.com/food-drink/
the-lobby-bar

OPENING HOURS:
Monday to Friday 8.00am–midnight,
Saturday 9.00am–midnight, Sunday
9.00am–10.30pm. Bar food served
daily 11.00am–11.00pm.

BOOKINGS:
Not taken

AGE RESTRICTION:
18+ after 8.00pm

**NEAREST UNDERGROUND
STATIONS:**
Charing Cross, Covent Garden

**PLACES OF
INTEREST NEARBY:**
Covent Garden, Royal Opera House,
Somerset House, The Courtauld
Gallery and Institute of Art,
London Transport Museum, Theatre
Museum, The British Museum,
London Film Museum, Theatre
Royal Drury Lane

the talented bar manager, Pedro Paulo, and
his team, and celebrates the theatricality of
London's great stage productions, many of
which have been performed in nearby Drury
Lane. The beautifully illustrated menu reads
like a theatre programme, introducing you
to the categories of cocktails, from light and
fresh in the 'Comedy' group, bubbly and
fruity for the 'Musical', unexpected blends of
sweet and sour for 'Satire', to the strong and
complex 'Drama' collection. Besides the list
of ingredients, you'll see which productions
inspired them, and, unusually, be provided with
a bar snack pairing recommendation.

The contemporary art collection throughout the hotel is exciting, none more so than the sculpted head of Dionysus, the Greek god of wine, in the Lobby Bar, and it is this that inspired the eponymous Comedy cocktail, sweet and tropical for a summer evening, filled with peach, rhubarb, and a hint of watermelon, and served in a replica container. If you are a musical lover, then you'll know exactly where the inspiration for Take a Chance on Me came from. Two of you can share this homage to the play 'Mamma Mia', as it comes in two halves, with the instruction 'If you change your mind, try the other half'. The finale to this collection are the 'Backstage' cocktails, one a not-to-be-missed immersive adventure, the other a tribute to the old fashioned, renamed One Fashioned, and made with great care from bourbon, tequila, or rum at the table.

If this list was not enough, there is, of course, the 'Lobby Bar Classics' list, for this bar never forgets its loyal clientele who return time and again to enjoy their favourite cocktails in a great bar.

Fairy Garden Infusion

Recipe courtesy of The Lobby Bar at One Aldwych

Inspired by *A Midsummer Night's Dream*, the Fairy Garden Infusion is a refreshing blend of Hendrick's Gin, Taylor's Chip Dry white port, coriander bitters, and rose lemonade. It is one of 17 'Showtime Cocktails' inspired by a West End or Broadway show, and it celebrates The Lobby Bar's location in the heart of Theatreland.

INGREDIENTS

- 50ml (1¾ oz) Hendrick's gin
- 30ml (1 oz) Taylor's Chip Dry white port
- 3 drops Bob's Bitters coriander bitters
- 100ml (3½ oz) rose lemonade
- Cucumber slice
- Fruit slices of choice
- Mint spring

METHOD

Combine the liquid ingredients and stir. Strain into a highball glass and garnish with a slice of cucumber and your choice of fruit (such as apple, grapefruit, and dragon fruit), then add a sprig of mint.

This recipe presents measurements for both UK and US readers. Units are given first for UK readers in the original measurement units, then for US readers in converted units in parentheses. Do not mix the units.

LONDON COCKTAIL CLUB (LIVERPOOL STREET)

This is just one of the nine themed London Cocktail Club locations found across the capital, each with its own distinctive style. The Liverpool Street bar is best described as a pleasure land carnival where you can join in all the fun of the fair. The themed basement bar is full of fairground fun, including Zoltar, the fortune-telling robot who famously made Tom Hanks' 13-year-old character into a 30-year-old man in the 1988 hit comedy *Big*. As a reminder of the Big Top, there are red-and-white-striped furnishings, optical illusion artwork, distortion mirrors, and in fact everything you'd find at the funfair or circus. This is a truly amusing place for any type of occasion, from after work drinks to chilling out with friends. You don't need to go far if you get peckish, as all the LCC bars are Deliveroo-friendly and encourage their customers to order in! Inside each of the VHS tapes, which are on every table, there are descriptions of nearby food venues, personalised to each bar, with their style of food.

So then, what of the cocktails, your reason for visiting? The 'LCC Legends' list includes the delicately flavoured Rose Petal Martini and the Jam Jar Daiquiri—served

in, you've guessed it, a jam jar, and topped with strawberry jam. There are also takes on the old favourites, like the Peanut Colada, a treat you are really going to go nuts for, and the Cherry Bomb Old Fashioned, balanced with Angostura and cherry bitters. Check the menu for the flavour of the month, all with labels that are prolific with puns, and look out for the sharing cocktails for 4, 8, or 10 people. It's always jolly good cocktails and jolly good fun at LCC.

There are many other LCC venues to suit your fancy, too, including locations in Covent Garden (Victoriana meets speakeasy), Monument (a basement bar beneath a not-quite Savile Row tailor's shop), Goodge Street (a heaven for punk rockers and gin lovers), Islington (a speakeasy where the hooch is hidden in medicine bottles), and Bethnal Green (Like Bacardi? Then head here for a Cuban cocktail on Paradise Row.).

ADDRESS:
206–210 Bishopsgate, Spitalfields, London EC2M 4NR

TEL: +44 (0)20 7580 1960

EMAIL:
liverpoolst@londoncocktailclub.co.uk

WEB: www.londoncocktailclub.co .uk/liverpool-street

OPENING HOURS:
Monday to Wednesday 4.00pm–midnight, Thursday 4.00pm–1.00am, Friday and Saturday 4.00pm–2.00am. Closed Sunday.

BOOKINGS:
Visit www.londoncocktailclub.co.uk/ bookings; phone reservation hours are Monday to Friday 10.00am–6.00pm, Saturday 10.00am–4.00pm

AGE RESTRICTION: 18+

EVENTS/LIVE MUSIC:
Monthly events; check the website

MASTERCLASSES:
Available for 2–25 people; visit www .londoncocktailclub.co.uk/masterclass

NEAREST UNDERGROUND STATIONS:
Liverpool Street

PLACES OF INTEREST NEARBY:
Heron Tower, Old Spitalfields Market, Dennis Severs' House, Brick Lane Market, Bank of England Museum, The Monument

LONG BAR

Sanderson

The stylish Phillippe Starck interior design of the luxury Sanderson hotel, right in the heart of London's West End, has been a talking point since it opened in 2000. Starck transformed the 1958, Grade II–listed building, creating a retreat from the hustle and bustle of city life and making it into a place where humour and fantasy are combined. The onyx Long Bar is just that, at some 24 metres (80 feet) in length, and is festooned above with striking displays of all manner of flora and greenery. Where better to people watch than seated at the bar on one of the quirky silver bar chairs, decorated with an all-seeing, surreal eye on the back? Alternatively, you can relax in the playful Courtyard Garden, and either way, you have a long list of cocktails to choose from.

There are two cocktails menus to peruse. All-time favourite 'Sanderson Classics' include a Deluxe Mojito, a gin-based Cucumber and Cinnamon, and a Jasmine Margarita, with citrus, pomegranate, and sal de gusano. The cutting-edge 'Signature' menu gives descriptions of the taste of each concoction, so you might go for

ADDRESS:
Sanderson, 50 Berners Street,
Fitzrovia, London W1T 3NG

TEL:
+44 (0)20 7300 5588

EMAIL:
london-guestservices@sbe.com

WEB:
www.morganshotelgroup.
com/originals/originals-
sanderson-london/eat-drink/
long-bar

OPENING HOURS:
Monday to Thursday
11.00am–1.00am, Friday and
Saturday 11.00am–2.00am, Sunday
11.00am–11.00pm

BOOKINGS:
Via the website

AGE RESTRICTION:
21+

EVENTS/LIVE MUSIC:
Varied; see description

**NEAREST UNDERGROUND
STATIONS:**
Tottenham Court Road, Goodge
Street

**PLACES OF
INTEREST NEARBY:**
Soho, Oxford Street, British
Museum, Covent Garden, Leicester
Square

the fresh, fruity, anise-flavoured Persephone, a mix of Grey Goose vodka, passion fruit, lime, pomegranate, and Prosecco. Or you might prefer a long, fresh, slightly spicy Japanese Whiskers, featuring soju, Suntory Toki whisky, passion fruit, lemon, lime, egg white, and paprika. If you are looking for a nightcap, then do order the smooth, herbal Imperium, created from Rémy Martin 1738, Italicus, Amontillado sherry, and lavender bitters. There are several good non-alcoholic cocktails listed too, and an excellent food menu with snacks and bigger bites to choose from. You can dance the weekend away, as there is live house and classics music every Friday and Saturday evening. Thursday nights swing to funky house and classics, and the first and third Wednesday of each month feature Sanderson Sessions, so check out the website for the DJ programme and to see who is on the decks.

THE MAYOR OF SCAREDY CAT TOWN

You'll have to tell the staff who greet you at The Breakfast Club that you are there to 'see the Mayor' before they let you in through the huge pink Smeg fridge door and direct you down the dimly lit stairs into the equally dimly lit brick-walled speakeasy cocktail bar. This underground bolthole is one of several eclectic Dirty Little Secret cocktail bars in London, and you need to be an avid fan of the American sitcom *Cheers*, which ran from 1982 to 1993, to know that the names of all of them are connected to the series. (In case you're curious, The Mayor appears in 'The Magnificent Six'.) This is cocktail heaven, and an excellent place for a date, as it's never too loud and the tables aren't on top of one another. The cocktail list is divided in two, with 'Dirty Little Specials', unique to each venue, and 'Dirty Little Regulars', available

ADDRESS:
12–16 Artillery Lane, Spitalfields,
London E1 7LS

TEL:
+44 (0)20 7078 9639

EMAIL:
henri@themayorofscaredycattown
.com

WEB:
www.themayorofscaredycattown.com

OPENING HOURS:
Monday to Thursday 5.00pm–
midnight, Friday 3.00pm–midnight,
Saturday 12.00pm–midnight, Sunday
12.00pm–10.30pm. Last entry
Monday to Wednesday 11.00pm,
Thursday to Saturday 11.30pm,
Sunday 10.00pm.

BOOKINGS:
Walk-ins welcome; first come,
first served. A handful of advance
bookings taken online.

AGE RESTRICTION:
18+

**NEAREST UNDERGROUND
STATIONS:**
Liverpool Street

**PLACES OF
INTEREST NEARBY:**
Old Spitalfields Market, Bishopsgate
Institute, Dennis Severs' House,
Brick Lane, Sandys Row Synagogue,
19 Princelet Street, Christ Church
Spitalfields

across all the bars. Return again and again for seasonally changing items. There's also a small food menu—and you can always eat upstairs in the all-day brekkie restaurant if you are really hungry. Leaving is as much fun as arriving. There's no fridge door this time—the exit takes you out through the toilets!

The other Dirty Little Secret bars in London are equally fun. Dr Kluger's Old Towne Tavern (in Canary Wharf) is a quirky downstairs bar, excellent for Aperol-based cocktails, with happy hour deals Monday to Friday from 5.00pm–7.00pm. Call Me Mr Lucky (in Southwark) is reasonably priced, and the cocktail list here concentrates on tequila. The place is quite fun, you'll need a password to get in, and it's another hidden treasure. The King of Ladies Man (in Battersea) is a cocktail bar and lounge hidden behind a wall, and is (intentionally) reminiscent of a 1970s bachelor pad, with some good snack food.

MR FOGG'S RESIDENCE

The Mayfair home of the late Phileas J. Fogg Esq., famed explorer and adventurer, is tucked away in a winding lane off Berkeley Square, where the doorman will greet you on the steps. When he has checked your reservation (it is a good idea to book, as it gets very busy), one of the amiable household staff will then invite you into the house, now a prestigious watering hole. It's a truly eccentric place, with wood-panelled walls and a huge fireplace, crammed from floor to ceiling with antiques, bric-a-brac, and artefacts collected during the course of Mr Fogg's Victorian era round-the-world travels. From birdcages, penny-farthing bicycles, stuffed parrots, and old books to a hot-air balloon, it's quirky and busy, with music—and sometimes live entertainment— that just about allows you to chat with your friends. The seating is comfortable, in the form of stools, upholstered seats, and armchairs by the 'fire'. Enjoy the complimentary

ADDRESS:
15 Bruton Lane, Mayfair, London
W1J 6JD

TEL:
+44 (0)20 7306 0608

EMAIL:
residence@mf-foggs.com

WEB:
www.mr-foggs.com/mr-foggs-residence

OPENING HOURS:
Monday to Friday 4.01pm–2.01am, Saturday 1.31pm–2.01am, Sunday 3.01pm–12.01am

BOOKINGS:
Visit www.sevenrooms.com/reservations/mrfoggsresidence

DRESS CODE:
Elegant and informal; no sportswear or scruffy trainers/sneakers

AGE RESTRICTION:
21+

NEAREST UNDERGROUND STATIONS:
Green Park, Bond Street, Oxford Circus, Piccadilly Circus

PLACES OF INTEREST NEARBY:
Green Park, Royal Academy of Arts, Burlington Arcade, Fortnum & Mason, Green Park

nibbles, which are kept topped up, or you can order light savoury and sweet snacks from the menu.

The extensive cocktail list is innovative and the signature menu, exclusive to Mr Fogg's Residence, takes you on a journey from London to Singapore and further afield. Spin the globe to find a drink concocted to recall where it all began. The £20,000 Wager, referring to a bet that was made at the Reform Club, is a mix of hibiscus-infused VII Hills gin, Sipsmith sloe gin, homemade raspberry leaf syrup, lemon juice, egg white, and rhubarb

bitters. Further into his journey, and yours, and having reached Singapore, you'll find Jungle Flora, containing chamomile-infused Russian Standard Platinum vodka, ginger liqueur, Chartreuse green herbal liqueur, fresh lime juice, egg white, homemade sugar syrup, and citrus foam. There is also the 'Estate' list, which has cocktails that are served at all Mr Fogg's venues. Whatever you choose, expect some very unusual presentations. The Residence oozes old world charm and is a highly engaging and amusing place where you can enjoy a jolly good drink.

The other Mr Fogg's locations are worth visiting as well. They include Mr Fogg's Society of Exploration (in the Strand), perfect for adventurous folk who enjoy a challenge. Mr Fogg's House of Botanicals (in Fitzrovia) is filled with masses of flora and fauna, collected by Mr Fogg on his expeditions. Mr Fogg's Gin Parlour (in Covent Garden) is proud home to one of the largest gin collections around; it's just the place for super gin cocktails, inspired by Mr Fogg's world travels.

THE NICKEL BAR

The Ned

Drinks are at the heart of The Nickel Bar, which serves both American staples and classic cocktails with a Ned twist from early morning until the wee hours. The bar is bang in the heart of the City of London inside The Ned, which takes its name from the architect, Sir Edwin 'Ned' Lutyens, who designed the building, back in the 1920s, as the headquarters of Midland Bank, then the largest clearing bank in the world. The massive ground floor has been skilfully converted, providing space for lots of restaurants as well as the magnificent marble-top centrepiece American bar. There is a real buzz here, and it may not be the place if you are looking for somewhere quiet to drown your sorrows, for the Nickel Stage—which was the bank's reception desk in a previous life—is alongside the bar and has a daily line-up of live performances. It

ADDRESS:
The Ned, 27 Poultry, City of London,
London EC2R 8AJ

TEL:
+44 (0)20 3828 2000

EMAIL:
restaurants@thened.com

WEB:
www.thened.com/restaurants/the-
nickel-bar

OPENING HOURS:
Monday to Friday 8.00am–2.00am,
Saturday 9.00am–3.00am, Sunday
9.00am–midnight

BOOKINGS:
Not taken

AGE RESTRICTION:
18+ after 8.00pm

EVENTS/LIVE MUSIC:
Daily; see the website for details

**NEAREST UNDERGROUND
STATIONS:**
Bank

**PLACES OF
INTEREST NEARBY:**
Bank of England Museum, The
Monument, Mansion House,
Guildhall Great Hall, Guildhall
Art Gallery, City of London Police
Museum, St Margaret Lothbury
Church, London Wall, Leadenhall
Market

tends to be quieter on weekends, when the City bankers have vacated their leather-upholstered wooden bar-side seats.

The cocktail list here is a tight offering of just twelve classics, timelined from 1900–2010, and aimed to please the busy crowd that flock here, and you'll be served by genial staff in crisp white shirts. The West Side Huricane is the bar's nod to the world famous New Orleans cocktail, which, rumour has it, was first served at the 1939 World's Fair in Queens at the Hurricane Bar. Eight-year-old rum is served long with pineapple, raspberry, and ginger beer, and the sophisticated addition of Averna provides a hint of bitterness to complement the fruit. Venice Beach is the liquid version of a sunny day in Florida: long and fruity, naughty but nice. Iced tea is one of the most popular thirst quenchers in the Southern United States, and here they use raspberry tea to add a refreshing hit of tannin and fruit. There's good food on offer to accompany your cocktail, too, with a small selection of bites available from midday—who can resist a turkey club sandwich or crispy fried latkes and apple sauce? The place positively vibrates with the music, the atmosphere is lively, and the drinks will cheer you up.

The Nedgroni

Recipe courtesy of The Nickel Bar at The Ned

The Nedgroni is The Ned's homage to one of the world's favourite drinks. Elegant Bombay Sapphire, stirred down bittersweet Kamm & Sons, a measure of vermouth, and a whisper of rose combine to create a drink that's complex and deep in flavour.

INGREDIENTS

- 25ml (1 oz) Bombay Sapphire gin
- 25ml (1 oz) Kamm & Sons British Aperitif (a bittersweet botanical spirit distilled with ginseng, fresh grapefruit peels, and manuka honey)
- 20ml (¾ oz) Martini Riserva Speciale Rubino vermouth
- 10ml (2 tsp) Lanique rose petal liqueur
- Grapefruit slice

METHOD

Stir the liquid ingredients with ice and serve in a rocks glass on ice. Garnish with a slice of grapefruit.

This recipe presents measurements for both UK and US readers. Units are given first for UK readers in the original measurement units, then for US readers in converted units in parentheses. Do not mix the units.

NIGHTJAR

Make a note of the door number before you arrive and you shouldn't find it too hard to locate the entrance to Nightjar. Otherwise, it's easy to miss the entrance with the very discreet Nightjar bird on the door of this fabulous speakeasy. It's also a very good idea to book, as walk-ins can be a bit limited. Whilst this is a really popular neighbourhood bar, the strong live music programme appeals to a much wider audience, pulling in visitors from far and wide. It's not too loud, and there is some nice booth seating for a bit of privacy. The cocktail list includes rare, revived, and original cocktails, so there is something for everyone. It's table service, which is nice, and if you are not sure what to order, then let the helpful, knowledgeable staff aid you.

The menu is divided into three groups, pre-Prohibition, Prohibition, and post-war, which cover the spectrum from early classics created by iconic bartenders, to serious cocktails from the desperate dry years, on to twists on modern day classics starting

ADDRESS:
129 City Road, Hoxton, London
EC1V 1JB

TEL:
+44 (0)20 7253 4101

EMAIL:
info@barnightjar.com

WEB:
www.barnightjar.com

OPENING HOURS:
Sunday to Wednesday 6.00pm–
1.00am, Thursday 6.00pm–2.00am,
Friday and Saturday 6.00pm–3.00am

BOOKINGS:
There are some walk-ins available,
but it is advisable to book. Via the
website or call Monday to Friday
12.00pm–5.00pm.

AGE RESTRICTION:
21+

EVENTS/LIVE MUSIC:
Daily from 9.30pm. Check the
website; some charges apply.

**NEAREST UNDERGROUND
STATIONS:**
Old Street

**PLACES OF
INTEREST NEARBY:**
XOYO, Wesley's Chapel and
Museum of Methodism

with the tiki age and into the new millennium
cocktail revival. If you are a two or more, then
have a look at the sharing section, which has
a selection of fun concoctions served up in
innovative containers. Take the Alchemist's
Brew, and you'll get a refreshing, malty, and
strong drink, a potent mix of Monkey Shoulder
whisky, The Kraken dark rum, Ceylon arrack,
with fruit juices, tea, and spices, which comes
served in a miniature copper pot still. There
are low-alcohol and non-alcoholic alternatives,
and a delicious menu of tapas and bar snacks to
round things off. Whether your drink is served
in a quirky container or a more conventional
glass, you are in for a treat.

ORIOLE

You'll find Oriole on an unlikely avenue in the historic Smithfield meat market, in the heart of the Square Mile of the City of London. There has been a livestock market on the site for more than 800 years, but if you want to catch the meat traders, you'll have to be here way before Oriole opens at 6.00pm. Think more about arriving at 7.00am Monday to Friday to find the full range of stalls open, and, if you are a tourist, come back after a day's sightseeing. But Oriole is an equally great place for Londoners to wind down after a hard day's work. You won't be disappointed, for once you have made it downstairs from the street, you'll be enchanted by the ambience and the warm hospitality, with table service from welcoming staff eager to please.

The album of mixed drinks, updated from time to time, takes you on a journey around the world, with stunning cocktails created to reflect the Old World, the

ADDRESS:
East Poultry Avenue, Smithfield
Market, Farringdon, London
EC1A 9LH

TEL:
+44 (0)20 3457 8099

EMAIL:
info@oriolebar.com

WEB:
www.oriolebar.com

OPENING HOURS:
Monday 6.00pm–11.00pm,
Tuesday to Sunday 6.00pm–late

BOOKINGS:
Walk-ins possible, but booking is
advised. Bookings can be made
online up to 90 days in advance.

AGE RESTRICTION:
21+

EVENTS/LIVE MUSIC:
Daily in the late evenings, with prices
ranging from free to £8. See the
website for details.

**NEAREST UNDERGROUND
STATIONS:**
Barbican, Farringdon

**PLACES OF
INTEREST NEARBY:**
Smithfield Market, Old Spitalfields
Market, Museum of London,
Postman's Park, Barbican Centre,
Central Criminal Court (Old Bailey),
St Paul's Cathedral, Guildhall Art
Gallery, St Bartholomew's Hospital

New World, and the Orient, all habitats of the exotic oriole bird. It's a real voyage of discovery: you might like to try Kiruna from Lapland, mixed from Absolut Elyx vodka, honey bread aquavit, mulberry leaf root cider, cloudberry jam, and lemon juice, giving you a sweet but earthy drink. If you are a whisky lover, then you might choose Skyefall, from the Isle of Skye in the Scottish Highlands. It's made with Talisker ten-year-old whisky, Freya Woodsmoke birch spirit, coffee leaf Chinato, espresso stout syrup, and, believe it or not, clarified octopus milk. (That's made by gently simmering actual octopus milk to draw out the flavour, and then clarifying the liquid so it loses its milky colour.) What you get is a smooth, almost buttery cocktail, with a touch of salted caramel and a hint of bitterness. If you prefer something fresh and zesty with a creamy finish, try the Chinese-influenced Cydonia Cup, mixed from Belvedere Pure vodka, gooseberry Rinomato Aperitivo, strawberry tree curd, and grapefruit juice. There are great cocktails for sharing, non-alcoholic cocktails mixed to order, and an exciting pan-Latin and Asian inspired bar food menu. Add a live music session to the mix and you won't want to leave.

OXO TOWER BAR

OXO Tower Bar, on the eighth floor of the iconic OXO Tower on the south bank of the River Thames, is the perfect spot for cocktails, whether it is after work, or pre- or post-theatre. On a fine day or evening, enjoy your drinks seated in the sunshine on the amazing 76-metre (250-foot) garden terrace, or watch the glittering city skyline seated at the comfortable bar. As well as the old favourites, the mixologist makes sure that you can find new cocktails at OXO and is always on the lookout for new pairings and flavours; there is a new cocktail showcased every month.

If you are feeling under the weather, what better than a dose of a cocktail labelled Penicillin, which combines Dewar's scotch, lemon, honey, and ginger with a splash of Laphroaig: not quite a bottled medicine, but it's sure to help get rid of chills and coughs. Perennially popular is the ultimate tiki concoction, Pleasure Boat, created

ADDRESS: 8th floor, OXO Tower, Barge House Street, South Bank, London SE1 9PH

TEL: +44 (0)20 7803 3888

EMAIL: oxo.reservations@harveynichols.com

WEB: www.harveynichols.com/restaurant/the-oxo-tower/bar

OPENING HOURS: Monday to Thursday 11.00am–11.00pm, Friday and Saturday 11.00am–midnight, Sunday 12.00pm–10.30pm

BOOKINGS: Available for drinks every day and evening except for Friday and Saturday nights. Via the website, or by telephone for parties of seven or more.

AGE RESTRICTION: 18+

EVENTS/LIVE MUSIC: Varied and changing monthly; see the website

MASTERCLASSES: Bespoke classes can be arranged for groups of 2–8; call or email oxo.events@harveynichols.com

NEAREST UNDERGROUND STATIONS: Southwark, Blackfriars, Waterloo, Embankment, Temple

PLACES OF INTEREST NEARBY: Tate Modern, Shakespeare's Globe, National Theatre, The Old Vic, Royal Festival Hall

from Bumbu rum and house orgeat shaken with fresh pineapple, passion fruit, lime, falernum, and aromatic bitters. The finishing touch is a float of fired Wood's 100 rum and nutmeg.

If you are feeling peckish, then don't miss the opportunity of enjoying a bite to eat from the cutting-edge menu. The bar food menu has a terrific list of small eats, from the simplest smoked almonds and Nocellara olives to, for example, a more substantial charcuterie board or beer-battered prawns with a soya and sesame dressing. There is a changing live music schedule every month, with lots of variety to make sure your weekends are filled with jazz, from King Swing and upbeat jazz to Brazilian samba folk. Check the website for what's on.

RADIO ROOFTOP BAR

ME London

High up above the Strand, with striking vistas across the River Thames and views of London's landmarks—think the London Eye, Big Ben, St Paul's Cathedral, and The Shard—Radio Rooftop Bar has become a premier rooftop destination for cocktails and more. It's refined and cool, and, not surprisingly, it can get very busy, so although you can take a chance and queue, to avoid disappointment it's wise to book in advance. You can make a request for a table on the terrace, which the team will do their best to accommodate. The dedicated lift (elevator) from the ground floor of the boutique hotel whisks you up to the 10th floor, where you'll be rewarded by entering a spectacular space, all bling, mirrored, and shiny, with extraordinary 360-degree views of the city's iconic skyline. The outside terrace has patio heaters and plush blankets for the faint-hearted, and the guests are as varied as the cocktails. There's a mini collection

ADDRESS:
10th floor, ME London, 336–337
Strand, Covent Garden, London
WC2R 1HA

TEL:
+44 (0)20 7395 3440

EMAIL:
London_Reservations@togrp.com

WEB:
www.radiorooftop.com/london

OPENING HOURS:
Monday to Wednesday
12.00pm–1.00am, Thursday
and Friday 12.00pm–2.00am,
Saturday 11.00am–2.00am,
Sunday 11.00am–midnight

BOOKINGS:
Recommended

DRESS CODE:
Smart casual

AGE RESTRICTION:
21+ after 5.00pm; hotel guests can be
18+ after 5.00pm

**NEAREST UNDERGROUND
STATIONS:**
Covent Garden, Leicester Square,
Charing Cross

**PLACES OF
INTEREST NEARBY:**
Covent Garden, Royal Opera House,
Somerset House, The Courtauld
Gallery and Institute of Art, London
Transport Museum, Theatre Museum,
British Museum, London Film
Museum, Theatre Royal Drury Lane

of 'Le Grand Fizz', all based on variations of
Grey Goose, St-Germain, and soda, a short list
of non-alcoholics, and a long list of seasonally
changing signature cocktails. Following the
radio theme, try the Radio Punch, a concoction
of Sailor Jerry spiced rum, manzana liqueur,
Chambord, lime, apple juice, and cantaloupe.
Or there's Radio Garden, which contains
Hendrick's gin, St-Germain, basil leaves,
cucumber, and elderflower. There is a variety of
sound, which changes from DJs to live music,
and there's sharing food of all sorts, from bar
snacks to small, medium, and large plates, as
well as dessert, so this can be the place for just
a drink or for the whole evening.

REVEREND JW SIMPSON

From the moment you step through the black front door of this themed Fitzrovia cocktail bar, you'll be struck by the originality of the place. Going down the stairs of this subterranean treasure, you'll find yourself in the former 'home' of Reverend Simpson, the fictitious former inhabitant. The ambience is cosy, and you get to enjoy your cocktails in one of the 'rooms' in his house on Goodge Street. Take a journey through the hallway, the living room, the kitchen, and the bedroom of the Reverend's previous abode, with cocktails inspired by each location. Hallway drinks are meant to whet your whistle on arrival, like the Welcome Maté, served long. The mix of Monkey Shoulder whisky shaken with peach liqueurs, fresh lemon and apple, and a splash of ChariTea sparkling maté is light and bright. You can be a Lounge Lizard in the living room, surrounded by knick-knacks and the Reverend's memorabilia. The kitchen is the heart of the house, and of the Reverend's soirées, with drinks to match the mood, and as you might expect from the bedroom, there's an appropriately named Nightcap: Merlet cognac with Drambuie and homemade blackberry shrub, topped with bubbles.

ADDRESS:
32 Goodge Street, Fitzrovia,
London W1T 2QJ

TEL:
+44 (0)20 3174 1155

EMAIL:
info@revjwsimpson.com

WEB:
www.revjwsimpson.com

OPENING HOURS:
Tuesday to Thursday 5.00pm–
midnight, Friday and Saturday
5.00pm–12.30am. Closed Sunday
and Monday.

BOOKINGS:
Via email

AGE RESTRICTION:
18+

MASTERCLASSES:
Available; check the website

**NEAREST UNDERGROUND
STATIONS:**
Goodge Street

**PLACES OF
INTEREST NEARBY:**
Grant Museum of Zoology, British
Museum, Pollock's Toy Museum

You can expect table service from welcoming staff who are happy to help you navigate the seasonal cocktail menu. The recipes are inventive and the presentation is innovative, but don't hesitate to ask for a one-off drink if you want it. It's a good spot for a date night, a terrific spot to drop in on the way home from work, and an excellent place to catch up with friends. Look out for special event dates as well as the 'Spirited Sermons' series of evening cocktail masterclasses, run by experienced bartenders who will guide you through the highs and lows of mixology. Music is from all over the record box, making this a really enjoyable place to stop for a drink.

THE RIVOLI BAR

The décor of the stylish Rivoli Bar dazzles with alabaster, illuminated Lalique glass panels, gold leaf, and glossy camphor wood clad walls, all of which capture the glamour and hedonism of the Art Deco era. It's an intimate cocktail lounge, an escape away from the hustle and bustle of Piccadilly and Mayfair, and is renowned as one of the best bars in Mayfair. The white-jacketed young bar staff are there to mix wonderful cocktails from an extensive and innovative menu, but are equally happy to customize a drink to your personal requirements. Seated at the bar, you can experience firsthand the magic of the mixologist as the cocktails are deftly created.

This is a place where tradition and innovation combine. The list of legendary classics includes Churchill's Courage, which pays homage to the late Sir Winston Churchill, who considered The Ritz as one of his favourite hotels. It's a bold mix of in-house, handcrafted, butter-washed Woodford Reserve bourbon, maple syrup, white port, vanilla bitters, and lemon peel, and is a testament to Churchill's leadership qualities and relationship with America. Or why not try a glass of the show-stopping Puttin' on the Ritz, inspired by the classic Fred Astaire song? The combination

ADDRESS:
The Ritz, 150 Piccadilly, St James's,
London W1J 9BR

TEL:
+44 (0)20 7300 2340

EMAIL:
dining@theritzlondon.com

WEB:
www.theritzlondon.com/dine-with-us/rivoli-bar

OPENING HOURS:
Monday to Saturday 11.30am–
11.30pm, Sunday 12.00pm–10.30pm

BOOKINGS:
Not taken

DRESS CODE:
Smart casual; trainers/sneakers and
sportswear are not permitted

AGE RESTRICTION:
Those under 16 may not sit at the bar

**NEAREST UNDERGROUND
STATIONS:**
Green Park

**PLACES OF
INTEREST NEARBY:**
Royal Academy of Arts, Green Park,
Savile Row, Burlington Arcade, Bond
Street, Piccadilly, Fortnum & Mason

of Chivas Regal 18 Years Old whisky,
Montenegro, Italicus, and cherry pomegranate
soda is sensational. The seasonal collection
incorporates creative homemade products,
besides which there are fabulous champagne
celebration cocktails, including the The Rivoli
75, a take on the all-time classic French 75.
The vintage Ritz cocktails are in a class of
their own, with price tags to match. That's not
surprising, as they combine long-forgotten
and unmatchable spirits, sourced from around
the globe. There is a fabulous caviar list and a
tempting array of delicious savories to share, as
well as sandwiches, salads, and desserts, and a
short but sweet non-alcoholic cocktail menu.
All the drinks will certainly exercise your credit
card, but this is a classic, and makes for a
memorable visit to a place where elegance and
refinement are the bywords.

Ritz 110

Recipe courtesy of The Rivoli Bar at The Ritz

This recipe is for one of The Ritz London's most famous cocktails. It was created in 2016 to celebrate The Ritz London's 110th year, and is a glamorous concoction containing pure gold, reflecting the lavish style.

INGREDIENTS

- 35ml (1¼ oz) Absolut Elyx vodka
- 25ml (¾ oz) Grand Marnier orange liqueur
- 50ml (1¾ oz) crème de pêche (peach liqueur)
- 110ml (3¾ oz) Ritz champagne
- 1 tsp gold leaves
- Orange peel
- Brown sugar cube

METHOD

Add all the liquid ingredients to a coupé glass. Top with gold leaves, which add sparkle to the glass. Decorate with twists of orange, which also add an amazing aroma to the drink. Finally, drop in a small cube of brown sugar to add fizz and make the cocktail even more appealing.

This recipe presents measurements for both UK and US readers. Units are given first for UK readers in the original measurement units, then for US readers in converted units in parentheses. Do not mix the units.

SCARFES BAR

Rosewood London

Now here is a really classy lounge bar with a great atmosphere, a favourite for end-of-the-working-day drinks, for a cocktail pre-theatre or pre-dinner, or just an excellent place to chill out any night of the week and enjoy the live jazz and wonderful vibe. The place has a welcoming, clubby feel about it, with leather chairs and sofas, walls lined with vintage books, rugs on the floor, cosy furnishings, and, of course, some of Gerald Scarfe's famous satirical cartoons adorning the marble-paneled walls. These transform the bar into a living canvas, described by Gerald as 'my personal art gallery, where you can see my life on these walls'.

Scarfes aims to offer something much more than just a cocktail, and has a themed menu that changes every year. Each drink is full of secrets and surprises, using carefully sourced ingredients. *Scarfes Bar Cocktail Book Vol. 1*, available to purchase, is

ADDRESS: Rosewood London,
252 High Holborn, Holborn,
London WC1V 7EN

TEL: +44 (0)20 3747 8611

EMAIL: info@scarfesbar.com

WEB: www.scarfesbar.com

OPENING HOURS:
Daily 4.00pm–1.00am

BOOKINGS: Not taken

AGE RESTRICTION:
18+ after 6.00pm

**NEAREST UNDERGROUND
STATIONS:** Holborn

**PLACES OF
INTEREST NEARBY:**
British Museum, Covent Garden, Sir
John Soane's Museum, Lincoln's Inn
Fields, Charles Dickens Museum,
The London Silver Vaults, Hunterian
Museum, Royal College of Surgeons,
Conway Hall, Somerset House

a work of art in itself. To start with, you get the lowdown on the groups of drinks, including sour and sweet, dry and bitter, fresh and floral, and fruity and spiced. The millennium-themed list was inspired by significant people and events since 2000. The cocktail Zingy Stardust represents 2002, with a memorable, zesty mix of two types of lime, including the rare juiceless zara lebu, lemongrass, and kaffir lime leaves, and silky Absolut Elyx. It's served straight up and finished with electric bitters to stimulate the taste buds, and the glass is adorned with a blue rim and Ziggy's iconic lighting bolt. For lovers of a long drink, then the High Wasted, a combination of Glenfiddich IPA, tobacco, hopped grapefruit, and coco and leather soda, has to be the drink for you. Paul McCartney was the hero for 2007, with a foamy, coffee-flavoured Macca-iato created in his name. Well-trained staff are on hand to help you decide on a beverage, complimentary nuts and a glass of water appear as if by magic, and there is nice bar food to enjoy alongside your cocktail. You won't be in a hurry to leave.

SEXY FISH

Anywhere that has a shoal of Frank Gehry glass fish floating overhead, a red lava stone bar, Damien Hirst mermaids, and a rain-effect window has to be a rather special destination. The bar at Sexy Fish is bold, opulent, and unashamedly glamorous, and it's just the place for people who want to be seen. On a warm evening, the doors are open onto Berkeley Square so guests can people-watch as they sip on a super cocktail. The cocktail menu, which sets out to whet the appetite and the senses, is eclectic and a work of art in itself, complete with a book of ambitious recipes for you to purchase and follow at home. There is a flavour map to help you choose the tipple to suit your mood. The rarest Japanese whiskies feature in some of the drinks, not surprising as the bar boasts at least 400 different labels and claims to have the largest collection in the world.

ADDRESS:
Berkeley Square House, Berkeley
Square, Mayfair, London W1J 6BR

TEL:
+44 (0)20 3764 2000

EMAIL:
N/A

WEB:
www.sexyfish.com

OPENING HOURS:
Monday to Saturday 12.00pm–
2.00am, Sunday 11.30am–1.30am

BOOKINGS:
Via the website

DRESS CODE:
Smart, chic, elegant, glamourous; no
branded sportswear, tracksuits, ripped
jeans, or flip-flops, but smart trainers/
sneakers are welcome

AGE RESTRICTION:
18+ in the bar; children under 18 are
allowed in the restaurant (but not the
bar) until 9.00pm

**NEAREST UNDERGROUND
STATIONS:**
Green Park

**PLACES OF
INTEREST NEARBY:**
Green Park, Royal Academy of Arts,
Burlington Arcade, Fortnum &
Mason

You could try the light and delicate
Japanese Kir, a gentle mix of falernum created
from a spiced-up Nikka From The Barrel
whisky, Grace koshu white wine, and soda
water. On the gin front, there is the curious
Neonach, a herbal and savoury concoction of
Hendrick's gin infused with smoked salmon,
basil, and fennel cordial garnished with chilli
oil. The menu offers perfect serves for both
cocktail novices and connoisseurs. Revamped
classics include the extravagant Rocky Road
Old Fashioned, which features buttered

Suntory Chita whisky, salt, chocolate, and a homemade biscuillate made with digestive biscuits, golden syrup, and vodka. There is sheer indulgence in the garnish of a mini marshmallow dipped in toffee sauce and digestive crumbs. Or try the dark and floral Monolith, created with Zacapa 23 rum, thyme, chamomile, balsamic, rosemary, and lavender. There is a small list of non-alcoholic cocktails, too, and as a bonus, with an eye on sustainability, the straws offered are completely biodegradable. If you are a brunch lover, then on any Sunday you could indulge in the fixed-price Sexy Brunch menu, which has its own additional cocktail list, notably including the signature Sexy Fish Bloody Mary, made from Absolut Elyx and spiced up with the house spice mix, tomato, and copper fish. Then add to the fun on Sunday evenings, when there is a live DJ set by Nick Grimshaw. This could be a hard place to resist visiting.

SWIFT

This is the ultimate in split personality bars; you get two for the price of one at Swift. The ground floor bar has more than a touch of Italian style about it, and is a buzzy and casual spot for a spontaneous drink, maybe on your way home from work or en route to the theatre in nearby Shaftesbury Avenue. The short list of drinks are affordable and on the lighter side, and include a refreshing, not-to-be-missed Sgroppino, a Prosecco-based drink, with citrusy Italicus and lemony sorbet floating on top. Or, for gin lovers, there is a marvelous Medallion, using lemongrass infused gin, grappa, lemon sherbet, mint, and absinthe. Of course, you can happily order any classic cocktail that you fancy.

The same applies downstairs, which is a different experience altogether: elegant, moody, and grown-up, where you will find knowledgeable, welcoming owners and staff. The lighting is low, the décor is a bit Art Deco meets East Asian, and the background music is not too loud. If you visit over the weekend, you have the added bonus of live

ADDRESS:
12 Old Compton Street, Soho,
London W1D 4TQ

TEL:
+44 (0)20 7437 7820

EMAIL:
info@barswift.com

WEB:
www.barswift.com

OPENING HOURS:
Monday to Saturday 3.00pm–
midnight, Sunday 3.00pm–10.30pm

BOOKINGS:
Upstairs bar is a standing, drop-in
bar. Downstairs bar bookings are
required and can be made for up to
13 people, online, by phone, or by
email.

AGE RESTRICTION:
20+

EVENTS/LIVE MUSIC:
Live music Friday and Saturday
9.00pm–11.00pm, Sunday
7.00pm–9.00pm

**NEAREST UNDERGROUND
STATIONS:**
Tottenham Court Road, Leicester
Square, Covent Garden, Piccadilly
Circus

**PLACES OF
INTEREST NEARBY:**
British Museum, Bloomsbury, Soho,
Theatreland, Covent Garden

blues and jazz music. You can happily while away the evening here, maybe on a date, or meeting up with friends. Sit at the bar and let the mixologists guide you, or choose one of the cosy semi-circular banquette booths and work your way through the longer, more serious menu of Swift cocktails and classics. If you favour a Negroni, then don't miss the house version, Ribbon, a sensational mix of Cocchi Storico Vermouth di Torino, Tio Pepe sherry instead of gin, and Campari with zesty Solerno, a Sicilian blood orange liqueur, to soften the bitter edge. Aside from great cocktails, there is a huge whisky list of well over 200 drams from around the world. And there is no need to go hungry, for there is a small but select food menu, featuring classic and Vietnamese oysters, a charcuterie selection, and a cheese board with the best that Neals Yard has to offer. You'll most certainly want to tell your friends about Swift, but remind them to make a reservation.

WHISTLING SHOP

The entrance to this low-lit, bare-brick cellar bar is easy to miss, but once you're inside, the place certainly gives you a sense of a bygone age, with its shabby-chic Victoriana-inspired décor, leather chairs and chesterfields, wooden tables, and oil lamps. There is plenty of space here, but if you want a bit more privacy, maybe for a date, then go for the recreated 18th-century dram shop. It's also used for the very popular Gin Masterclasses, which introduce you to the stories behind the drinks and the ingredients as well as guiding you through making the cocktails. Look out for the bathtub filled with botanicals, a tribute to the early 18th century, when the craze for drinking gin swept the lower classes off their feet and found them filling tubs like this with cheap adulterated spirit and flavouring it with whatever herbs and spices they could lay their hands on.

ADDRESS:
63 Worship Street, Shoreditch,
London EC2A 2DU

TEL:
+44 (0)20 7247 0015

EMAIL:
info@whistlingshop.com

WEB:
www.whistlingshop.com

OPENING HOURS:
Monday and Tuesday 5.00pm–
midnight, Wednesday and Thursday
5.00pm–1.00am, Friday and Saturday
5.00pm–2.00am. Closed Sunday.

BOOKINGS:
Not essential, but advisable if you
want a table. Seats at the bar are
non-reservable.

AGE RESTRICTION:
18+

MASTERCLASSES:
Available for 2–12 people. Inquire via
the website or email.

**NEAREST UNDERGROUND
STATIONS:**
Moorgate, Liverpool Street, Old
Street

**PLACES OF
INTEREST NEARBY:**
Wesley's Chapel and Museum of
Methodism, Bunhill Fields, British
Red Cross Museum, Barbican Centre

The seasonally changing list of cocktails
is inspired by the Victorian and Dickensian
drinking culture and is the result of months
of in-house experimentation in the Lab
distillery. The outcome is cocktails that can
tend toward the theatrical—sit at the bar and
see the smoke rise from some. Every single
one is also offered as a traditional or non-
alcoholic drink. Featured drinks have included
Mr Merdle, named after a Dickens character
in *Little Dorrit*, a short, bright drink made of
cognac, calvados, quince lemon, cinnamon, and
sage. There's a long, floral number, Columbia
Road, appropriately named after the nearby
flower market, which combines gin, ginseng,
lemon, lavender, honey, and soda. Traditional
bar nibbles, a cheese board, and a selection of
cured sausages from Borough Market make up
the food menu. Add the music, which is usually
upbeat jazz, electro jazz, blues, or soul, any of
which liven up the already terrific atmosphere,
and you've got a good place for a date, for a
friends get-together, or just for a stop-off on
the way home from work.

Credits

All images courtesy and copyright of the respective venues in the book, except as follows: pages 14, 16, and 17, Niall Clutton (for 12th Knot/Sea Containers London); page 23, David Loftus (for American Bar/The Beaumont); pages 5, 7 bottom left, and 24, @canon_photos (for American Bar/The Savoy); page 62, David Griffen (for Blind Spot/St Martins Lane); pages 111 and 112, Charlie McKay (for Little Bat); page 125, Jade Nina Sarkhel (for The Mayor of Scaredy Cat Town); page 139, Jerome Courtial (for Nightjar); pages 136 and 137, Edmund Weil (for Nightjar); pages 140, 141, and 143, Elena Bolster (for Oriole); pages 148, 149, and 150, Chris Orange (for Radio Rooftop Bar/ME London); pages 158 and 160, Addie Chinn (for Scarfes Bar/Rosewood London); page 167, Elena Bolster (for Swift); pages 166, 168, and 169, David Ryle (for Swift).

Miscellaneous images courtesy and copyright of the respective venues and photographers: front cover, The Nickel Bar/The Ned; back cover top, OXO Tower Bar; page 2, Mr Fogg's Residence; page 5, @canon_photos (for American Bar/The Savoy); page 6, Blue Bar/The Berkeley; page 7 bottom left, @canon_photos (for American Bar/The Savoy); page 7 right, Connaught Bar/The Connaught; page 7 top left, Callooh Callay; page 8 left, Balthazar; page 8 right, Mr Fogg's Residence; page 9 right, Balthazar; page 10 bottom left, Long Bar/Sanderson; page 10 top left, Bourne & Hollingsworth Buildings; page 10 top right, The Lobby Bar/One Aldwych; page 10 bottom middle, Donovan Bar/Brown's Hotel; page 10 bottom right, Blue Bar/The Berkeley; page 11 left, Chris Orange (for Radio Rooftop Bar/ME London); page 11 right, American Bar/The Stafford.

About the Author

Susan Cohen is a born and bred Londoner, with a love of the social and cultural history of the capital. She is an experienced author, and has written *London's Afternoon Teas*, the definitive guide to the very best places in London for afternoon tea. Her other books cover a wide range of social history subjects, and include *The District Nurse*, *The Women's Institute*, *Medical Services in the First World War*, *The Scouts* and *1960s Britain*. Susan often gives talks to a variety of audiences and has contributed many articles to a number of journals. When she is not writing, she practices Pilates and regularly goes hiking in the countryside.

Index